INDOOR GARDENING

&

GREENHOUSE

A Complete Guide to Cultivating Fruits, Vegetables and Herbs for Beginners

TOM GORDON

© **Copyright 2020 - All rights reserved.**

The content contained within this book may not be reproduced, duplicated or transmitted without direct written permission from the author or the publisher.

Under no circumstances will any blame or legal responsibility be held against the publisher, or author, for any damages, reparation, or monetary loss due to the information contained within this book. Either directly or indirectly.

Legal Notice:

This book is copyright protected. This book is only for personal use. You cannot amend, distribute, sell, use, quote or paraphrase any part, or the content within this book, without the consent of the author or publisher.

Disclaimer Notice:

Please note the information contained within this document is for educational and entertainment purposes only. All effort has been executed to present accurate, up to date, and reliable, complete information. No warranties of any kind are declared or implied. Readers acknowledge that the author is not engaging in the rendering of legal, financial, medical or professional advice. The content within this book has been derived from various sources. Please consult a licensed professional before attempting any techniques outlined in this book.

By reading this document, the reader agrees that under no circumstances is the author responsible for any losses, direct or indirect, which are incurred as a result of the use of information contained within this document, including, but not limited to, — errors, omissions, or inaccuracies.

Table of Contents

Indoor Gardening 1

    Introduction 2
    Chapter One - Where To Grow Your Garden Indoors 7
    Chapter Two - Getting Started Gardening 23
    Chapter Three - The Operation Cycle Of An Indoor Garden 44
    Chapter Four - Growing Beautiful Fruits 63
    Chapter Five - Cultivating Delicious Vegetables 90
    Chapter Six - Planting Healthy Herbs 107
    Chapter Seven - Common Mistakes And How To Avoid Them 126
    Final Words 138

Greenhouse 140

    Introduction 143
    Chapter One - Greenhouse Gardening 144
    Chapter Two - Operating A Greenhouse 182
    Chapter Three - Greenhouse Equipment 194
    Chapter Four - Cultivating Fruits 210
    Chapter Five - Cultivating Vegetables 230
    Chapter Six - Cultivating Herbs 259
    Chapter Seven - Maintaining Your Greenhouse 282
    Chapter Eight - Pests And Disease Control 301
    Chapter Nine - Mistakes To Avoid 325
    Final Words 333

INDOOR GARDENING

Learning How to Grow Fruits, Vegetables and Herbs for Beginners

By Tom Gordon

INDOOR GARDENING

INTRODUCTION

INDOOR GARDENING

More and more people are getting into gardening every day. With the current focus on living green and eco-friendly lifestyles, gardening has become cool again. Some people enjoy doing their part to help the environment, others enjoy the feeling of taking care of a living organism, and others simply want to grow their own fruits, vegetables, and herbs. There are only a few things in this life as satisfying as a home-cooked meal with fresh ingredients you grew yourself. Plus, when you grow yourself you can be sure that no harmful chemicals have slipped into your meals.

When most people hear the word gardening, they think of a plot of land with a little farm or the corner of a backyard that has been converted into a vegetable patch. Gardening seems to go hand in hand with the outdoors. They have been traditionally paired together, a staple of many North American paintings and stories. But here in the 21st century, it can take a lot of work to get access to land for gardening. Some cities have communal gardens where you can rent a space but this option doesn't fit everyone. With more people living in apartment buildings than ever before, we find the need to expand how we consider gardening. It is time to embrace the indoor garden.

If you're reading this introduction, then there's a good chance that you are ready to start your indoor garden, but you just don't know how yet. Don't worry, this book will cover everything you need to get set up and start growing your own fruits and vegetables. But there is also the possibility that you haven't decided if indoor gardening is right for you yet. This is understandable, as there are just as many cons to indoor gardening as there are pros. Let's take a look at the good and the bad of indoor gardening so you can weigh both sides and decide if it is right for you.

Let's begin with the pros. Indoor gardening allows more people to take part and join the gardening wave that is sweeping through the culture. Because of a lack of access to ground to plant a garden outdoors, indoor gardening may be a necessity for those that want to garden. But that necessity also allows for a lot of flexibility. Planting in the ground, you know exactly where your plants need to go. But an indoor garden can be done on a bookshelf, a dedicated space for a hydroponic setup, or even in hanging baskets around the living room. In this manner, indoor gardening actually allows for quite a variety of approaches.

You are also able to fully take control of the environment in which your garden is raised. From setting up lights to provide heat, establishing fans to keep the air fresh, and arranging plenty of water, you are able to fine-tune your garden in much greater depth when it is indoors. If you have an outdoor garden that needs a lot of light, then an overcast day can do serious harm to your plants. But an indoor garden uses electric lights to simulate the sun, and that means it doesn't matter if it is sunny, overcast or raining, your plants are always under your control. This level of control, when respected and utilized with intention, also means you can avoid issues with pests and disease much easier than you could with an outdoor garden. However, that will lead us into our first con as well.

Just because it is easier to avoid pests and disease when gardening indoors doesn't mean that they aren't still an issue. In fact, when pests take to an indoor garden, it can be even harder to repel them than if they were outdoors. Predatory insects seem even less appealing when you're looking at releasing them into your living room, after all! If you are going to garden indoors, then you need to make sure you keep your garden clean and tidy, well-fed, and properly protected. All of this equals more chores around the house on a daily basis. This means time and energy have to be committed to the garden's upkeep, time and energy that you may not feel compelled to give after a long day at work.

Other problems that indoor gardens face are a bit cuter. If you have children or pets, then you could run into problems with keeping your garden safe. Children have a tendency to break just about everything they get their hands on, and pets, such as cats, may use your garden as a litter box or even get sick (and possibly die) from chewing on the plants you are growing. What this means is that if you have children or pets, then you need to consider the security of your garden much more deeply than you would if it were outdoors.

While an indoor garden offers control over the environmental factors at play, these can prove to be difficult to keep in check when put in practice. Making sure that the temperature and lighting your plants need is correct may take up more time than you imagine. This is true even when these elements are automated. Automating your garden isn't an excuse to ignore your garden. The biggest con yet though, is that even if you take care of all of these, even if you make sure to battle pests and keep the environment in check, you may still find that your plants just aren't as tasty as those grown outdoors. Making sure you look after everything properly should keep this from being too big an issue, but many growers find they can taste the difference between an indoor or an outdoor tomato.

Those are the pros and cons. You may notice that many of the cons are only negatives when they are compared with outdoor gardening. If you don't have the option to choose between indoor and outdoor, then that con list should look quite a bit smaller. The fact of the matter is that an indoor garden is absolutely more fun and enjoyable than having no garden at all. So if you are ready to start raising delicious fruits, vegetables, and herbs in your home, then flip the page to get started!

CHAPTER ONE

WHERE TO GROW YOUR GARDEN INDOORS

When it comes to growing a garden indoors, the first step is to prepare the space necessary for your growing operation. You may only want a couple of plants hanging up in your living room, or you might want to dedicate a room of your apartment to act as your personal greenhouse. Regardless of which you choose, it is important to consider the space itself. Will your plants get enough sun there, or will you need to invest in lights? Will you have access to all of your plants in this design, or are there some you won't be able to reach? Are the temperature and humidity going to be manageable there?

Starting with these questions first is important as it allows you to get a good sense of your growing operation before you even spend a dollar. Questions about sunlight and humidity might be best answered when you know what kinds of fruits and vegetables you want to plant rather than just guessing the answers. If you already know what you want to plant, then you can follow the directions for the best humidity and hours of daylight they'll need. If you aren't fully sure what you want to plant, you don't need to worry. The advice covered in this chapter will ensure that you pick the best possible spot for your garden.

Working with Available Space

You don't need to go out and rent a new apartment or greenhouse just to have an indoor garden. Chances are you have plenty of space available to you right this second if you use it properly. Bookcases, windowsills, hanging plants, you can fit a whole vegetable garden into your living room with a little bit of creativity. Of course, if you want to go big, then we're going to address that as well. But it is important to keep in mind that it really doesn't take up a lot of space to start gardening. You could even spread your garden out between rooms if you had to: keep your tomatoes in the living room while your lettuce is in the bedroom. The only thing stopping you is the limits of your imagination. In this section, we are going to make the assumption that you're looking to do a little bigger setup than this, enough that you will need to consider the space more objectively. However, keep in mind that many of the tips for larger growing operations are equally applicable to smaller ones as well.

When it comes to picking the right space for your garden, it is important to consider how much sunlight the room gets and how much control you have over both the humidity and the temperature of the space. These three points will be discussed in more detail in a moment, but you should keep them in mind when deciding what location to use. If you find that you are going to need equipment such as a dehumidifier or grow lamps, then you need to dedicate a larger space to the grow than if you can rely on the natural features of the space. It can be a good idea to sketch out the area you are looking to grow and to take notes on all of these different elements. When you have them all down on paper in front of you, you may find that the space isn't as ideal as you first thought.

INDOOR GARDENING

Regardless of where you choose, you are going to want to make sure it can be properly set up to maintain your plants with minimal exposure to the risk of disease and infestation. Some gardeners like to set up their plants behind security measures such as a zippered airlock to help minimize risk. This is especially true for those that choose to grow using a hydroponic method, though we will be focusing our attention on soil-grown plants. Since this is the case, our best bet in reducing infection is to ensure that we use an area with proper flooring and good ventilation to promote healthy airflow.

Flooring may seem like an odd choice to focus on when you consider that our plants will be in pots, and therefore not touching the floor. There are two reasons that we want to keep flooring in mind. The first is the reduction of risk and this means that you should avoid setting up your garden in a carpeted space. For one, carpets can get damaged and even begin to grow mold due to spills during watering. Carpets also catch and hold onto a lot of bacteria and germs, and this is very unhealthy for your plants. Mold is going to be something you need to watch out for in general when it comes to your plants; for example, part of maintaining your garden is removing dead plant matter that can then rot and mold and spread disease. It is a lot harder to tell that there is a problem with your carpet than it is to remove fallen plant matter. Some people dislike setting up their gardens in a room with a wooden floor because watering can cause damage to it as well. However, you can minimize this risk by setting up a tarp for your plants to rest on. Just make sure the tarp can easily be cleaned, and you have a way to remove any spilled water. The biggest recommendations for flooring are slate, linoleum or ceramic, though we don't always have the option to choose one of these.

Airflow is vital to your plants. You probably know that your plants can drown when overwatered. It might sound a little weird to hear, but did you know that your plants can suffocate, too? When you're in a stuffy room, you begin to overheat and lose your breath, right? This can happen to your plants as well. Their leaves will let go of moisture, almost like they were sweating. A little bit of this is perfectly normal; in fact, it is what allows your plants to gather more water from the soil. But if they get too hot, too stuffy, then they can't breathe the air anymore and they begin to wilt and die. This needs to be considered when choosing your growing space. You might be able to fit a few plants and the necessary lights into that broom closet of yours, but the lack of airflow could leave you with a bunch of dead plants. You need to either have a natural airflow that they can benefit from or provide them with fans to keep the air circulating.

A healthy circulation of air does more than just keep your plants alive, though. Proper ventilation and airflow will see a reduction in harmful bacteria and mold that can cause disease; it will also help to make it harder for pests to take up home on your plants. Due to the small size of many garden pests, the airflow will make it difficult for them to properly control their bodies to land on your plants. That same breeze that makes it harder for pests to land can help your plants in their pollination phase, though chances are you won't have to worry about this since you're focusing on fruits, vegetables, and herbs. What's more important than the assistance with pollination is the fact that a decent breeze will strengthen your plants. Branches will grow stronger due to the breeze, and this will promote root growth and lead to better harvests. Plants need CO_2 in the air in order to best grow. When in a room with stale air, they will suck up all the CO_2 and then start to suffocate. Healthy airflow will bring plenty of fresh CO_2 and oxygen into your grow space so that you can have healthy, high yielding plants. Plus, airflow will help in keeping the temperature and humidity levels in check. So when you are planning your space, pay attention to the way that the air moves through the area. If it doesn't, then you are going to have to invest in some fans and these will take up space, so it is best to plan around them early.

Finally, we will be talking about sunlight more in depth in a moment but it needs to be considered here as well. Plants need light; it is pretty much a rule of thumb with all plants unless you are purposefully growing something with very unusual needs. When considering the space, pay attention to the sunlight it will get. Growing indoors often means you can't rely purely on sunlight but rather need to purchase grow lights. Like all equipment, these take up space that should be planned for. Grow lights also eat up electricity and this means a monetary cost is associated with them. Your best option is likely to use a combination of sunlight and electric illumination. Basically, this means that you find out how much sun the space gets and then use the lights to give your plants the extra boost they need. For example, tomatoes need at least eight hours of light. If you can rely on the sunlight for six hours of the day then you only need to prove another two or three hours of light through your gear. Gardening indoors often requires this sort of flexibility to ensure a delicious harvest.

Using Natural Sunlight

When we garden outdoors, we obviously trust the sun to provide our plants with everything they need. There may be overcast or rainy days that cause issues, but we typically don't set up lights to compensate for these. We give our trust over completely to the natural order of things. However, when it comes to indoor gardening, this becomes much trickier. Our access to the sun is dependent on windows, doorways, and the like. We can still make use of the sun but it is going to take more consideration than simply planting in the backyard and letting nature take its course. In order to best make use of our glowing orange globe, let's take a moment to consider how it moves in relation to your gardening space.

INDOOR GARDENING

The first thing to remember is that the sun rises in the east and sets in the west. Since this happens every single day, we can use this to set up an experiment to see how much sun we can capture indoors. But in order to do this, you need to first figure out which direction your apartment or house is facing. One way to do this is to grab a compass and see which direction each wall is in. If you don't have a compass, don't worry, you can do this from the comfort of your computer chair. Go to maps.google.com and input your address. Click on the satellite view button and you'll see that the view includes a compass in the corner. You can use this to see exactly which way everything is facing and use this to help you determine the best location for your garden to get plenty of sun. But hold up, there's one more important step.

If you live in the Northern Hemisphere, then the winter sun will rise in the southeast, head more south, and then set in the southwest. This leaves the sun on the south side throughout the day. The summer sun will rise in the northeast and travel over to the northwest, leaving it more on the north side of the house throughout the day. Knowing this, you can judge whether you want to plant facing the north or the south. So now we know how the sun travels and which section of your dwelling it is going to be at, but this still doesn't fully capture everything you need. There is one last step that you need to consider: the environment around you.

Take a look out of the windows in the grow space you are considering. If you live in the city, you may have buildings that are blocking out part of the sun's path; if you dwell in the country, then you may have trees and foliage that cast shade. Depending on how they block the sun's path, these could cause major issues. As an example, if you have a building that stops sunlight from getting to your plants for two hours of the day, then this can certainly be harmful to your plants. Just like you and I need our sleep, and our bodies tend to set their rhythms based on how much light is around us, so too do plants. When they lose the light for those hours, they will think it is time to sleep. This will lead to a rude awakening when they are suddenly hit with a strong burst of sunlight two hours later. It may seem silly to worry about the sleep patterns of your plants, but this affects them adversely and leads to health complications and a reduction in yield.

By taking the time to research the sun's relationship with your grow space, you will be able to identify possible issues such as this ahead of time. One solution to this particular problem would be to invest in some grow lights and an automatic timer. You can set the timer so the lights come on fifteen minutes before the sun disappears behind the obstruction, and turn off fifteen minutes after it peeks back out. As the arc of the sun changes throughout the year, it is useful to keep track of what it is doing so that you can adjust the required time as necessary. By setting it up to have a fifteen minute window of overlap, you create a safety buffer to ensure that your plants always get the light they need to stay healthy and strong.

Thinking about Temperature and Humidity Control

The final piece that you need to consider in this planning stage is that of the temperature and the humidity of the grow space. Different plants require different temperatures and humidity levels, which means that you may need to consider a second grow space if you are looking to produce something completely out of sync with the majority of your garden.

That said, you can almost certainly bet that whichever space you pick will need to have more humidity added to it. Plants just love the stuff. Remember how we

INDOOR GARDENING

mentioned that plants breathe? The pores from which they breathe lose moisture when the air around them is dry. This can leave the plants shriveled up and dead very quickly. A good rule of thumb when it comes to plants is the thicker the plant's leaves are, the less humidity it will require. The humidity for an indoor vegetable garden should be around the 40%-50% range. If you don't know the humidity of your grow space, you can purchase a hygrometer at most drugstores. These handy little devices will let you monitor indoor humidity.

Hygrometer in hand, check the grow space throughout the day. While going in and just getting a single rating may do the trick, it is always best to have an idea of how the space changes throughout the day. The space will probably need to have humidity added to it, which you

INDOOR GARDENING

can do by setting up a humidifier. But don't forget, every new piece of equipment you need to add to your garden will require space. It is important to bear that in mind so that you always reach each and every plant. Cutting off access to a plant almost guarantees that you'll neglect to give it the care it needs. With the new humidifier, you can set a timer to keep the humidity in check at all times, thanks to the notes you took with the hygrometer.

A vast majority of the vegetables you are likely to grow will require a temperature of 65-75F. Plants won't immediately die if they are slightly off from their preferred temperature. You can most likely keep alive one that wants 65F while growing those that want 75F, but the yield will reflect this.

Go out and grab yourself an indoor thermometer. There are some that can be programmed to record the temperature at set intervals; such an instrument could be a worthwhile investment. As with the humidity, you want to keep track of the temperature of your chosen space throughout the day. It is obviously going to fluctuate greatly as the day changes to night. A top-range thermometer will let you see if you need to add heaters or fans to adjust the temperature of the room. You will want to have a fan going, so remember to take the temperature both with and without that being active. If you have yet to get the fan, then you can adjust these numbers later on. The important thing is to keep track of them so that you always know exactly what is

INDOOR GARDENING

happening with your plants. This level of attention may seem unnecessary, but your garden's yield will show you why it pays to treat your plants well.

Chapter Summary

- With a little creativity, you can grow vegetables all around your house. Bookshelves, window ledges, and hanging pots are all options available for would-be gardeners short on space!

- It is likely though that you will want to set aside a designated space for your garden. This will make it easier to maintain proper temperature, humidity, and light control. It will also reduce the risk of plants getting infected by harmful bacteria.

- Some indoor gardeners like to set aside a room for their plants or raise them in tents. That's a good idea; it reduces the chance of infection and keeps them safe.

- You want to ensure that your grow space is ventilated and that it has a decent airflow, either naturally or by purchasing a fan. This will help to reduce the risk of infestation and promote healthy growth. It will also prevent your plants from suffocating!

- Your growing space should not be on a carpeted floor. Carpets capture lots of bacteria and they can easily be water damaged. A wooden surface is all right if you can put down a tarp first, but the best options are slate, linoleum, or ceramic flooring.

INDOOR GARDENING

- Even if you're able to make use of natural sunlight to light your plants, the chances are good that you will still need to purchase a few grow lights. Always remember to calculate space for equipment as well as for plants. You want to be able to reach all your plants to give them proper care.

- Find out which direction your apartment or house faces to decide where you can expect sunlight to come from throughout the year.

- Natural sunlight is great for your plants, but there are many things that can obstruct its pathway to your garden. Learning how much sun your room is getting is important, as you may need to supplement natural lighting with artificial lighting so that your plants get enough to survive.

- Because of the way their pores work, plants need to have moisture in the air. Without it, they begin to suffocate and die. You want the humidity in your grow space to rest around 40%-50%. There is a good chance that you will need to use a humidifier for this.

- Most vegetables also want a temperature between 65-75F. Use a thermometer to track the temperature of your space to get a sense of how much you need to raise or lower the temperature. Don't forget that you will be using a fan in the area, as well as lights.

INDOOR GARDENING

In the next chapter, you will learn how to choose the right container for your plants to live and grow. You'll also learn more about the different materials and tools you'll need to look after your vegetable or fruit garden. From lights to fans, soil to shears, you'll have everything you need to start and care for your personal indoor garden.

CHAPTER TWO

GETTING STARTED GARDENING

Now that you have chosen a space for your garden, it is time to start gathering all of the necessary materials and putting them together. We'll talk about the tools discussed in the last chapter, the fans and humidifiers. However, we'll primarily be talking about the containers which home our plants, the growing medium that they live in, and the various tools that we use to look after them and keep them healthy.

By the end of this chapter, you should be able to put together a shopping list for all the items you need to look after your garden. In creating this list, it is worthwhile to note that we are not looking at the supplies necessary for growing a hydroponic garden. While hydroponic gardens function perfectly well indoors, they have an entirely different set of needs than the plants we are raising in this garden. We're getting our hands dirty in the soil just like people used to!

Picking the Right Container for Your Plants

There are two steps to picking the perfect container for your plants. The first is to consider the size of container that type of plant needs. We'll first take a quick look at the different sizes and what they are used to grow. But the other step is to consider the material that the container is made out of. Once you have figured out what is right for your needs, there will still be one last step you should consider when making your list.

Pots come in all different sizes. At the lower end are tiny 10-inch pots. On the higher end are your 30-inch ones or 3 gallons on the small end and 30 gallons on the high. You also have 14, 16, 18 and 24 inch pots which are typically used. If you go after unique shapes and designs, then you may end up with oddly shaped pots that don't line up with these. By focusing our attention on these sizes, you will be able to see the difference between them

INDOOR GARDENING

and use that knowledge to make an educated guess on what you can grow in any weird pots you end up with. Trust me, once you get gardening, people have a tendency to give you pots as gifts.

10-inch: In a pot as small as this, you can only grow a herb like mint or sage. Or you could grow a single strawberry or head of leaf lettuce. You could go crazy and grow four turnips or a dozen French carrots but that's pretty much it.

14-inch: One cabbage, four peas, a single collard. You can go crazy here and plant ten carrots, regular-sized ones instead of the smaller French rounds. You could probably get away with three heads of leaf lettuce. Four if you're careful.

16-inch: Now you can really get away with growing some great vegetables. You can fit everything from before but now in greater quantity. However, this is still too small for many vegetables.

18-inch: There's a good chance that you'll be looking at pots of this size or higher for your garden. This is because one of these can house an eggplant, a pepper, a cauliflower, a tomato bush, or broccoli. Still, it can only fit one of those because they're bigger plants.

24-inch: You can grow cucumbers, blackberries, raspberries, vining tomatoes, squash, or even a fig tree with a 24-inch pot. Again, you'll only be growing one of these per pot.

30-inch: Chances are you'll only use a 30-inch container if you want to grow really large and heavy plants such as cherry trees, sweet corn, pumpkins, or rhubarb.

Using this guide to plan out what pots you need, you should be able to settle on some sizes now. So let's turn our attention over to the material. The most popular choices are between plastic, wood, terracotta, or ceramic. Each of these has its pros and cons. However, you need to make sure that whatever kind you go with has built-in drainage so that you don't drown your plants.

Right off, you should probably avoid wooden pots. While these are popular for many growers, they do have their drawbacks. For one, they will slowly break apart over time. They also can rot from water damage, which isn't ideal when you consider how much plants enjoy their water. Ceramic is a better choice than wood and often looks quite beautiful and brightly colored. They're great for indoor plants but they are one of the most expensive options.

If you are concerned about price, then terracotta or plastic might prove more affordable than ceramic. Plastic containers are very light, which makes it easier to move your plants. However, this can lead to issues if you are looking to grow heavy plants. Plastic tends to be the cheapest to purchase, though they are prone to breaking down just as much, if not more, than wooden pots. Terracotta, on the other hand, is cheaper than ceramic but more expensive than plastic. It is also much heavier than plastic. Terracotta pots have a tendency to dry quicker than the other kinds, so, if you use them, you will need to water your plants more often. Of course, if you are growing some herbs that enjoy dryer climes, then this can be a blessing.

Regardless of which you go with, you can expect each category to sell at a range of prices depending on how fancy the pot is. You can easily spend a couple of hundred dollars on pots that could be bought for $20 in a cheaper design. Your plant will enjoy a boring container just as much as they do a pretty one, so this is all about what you want rather than what the plant needs.

There is one more thing about containers that should be addressed. It is a smart idea to purchase some smaller ones which you can use for planting seeds. When you plant a seed, you do so in a smaller container, and then move it to its larger home when it has grown to a healthy size. Having some smaller containers around is always a good idea. Just as you'll end up being given pots as a gift, people also will start giving you seeds. You never know when you might have a new vegetable joining your garden.

Picking the Perfect Soil

There are all sorts of different kits out there with marketing that tells you exactly why you should use their soil and only their soil. This can make it seem like choosing the right type is a stressful experience. The truth of the matter is it doesn't have to be stressful at all. If you care about the taste of your vegetables, then you must use an organic potting mix. You can go to any gardening store and say, "I'm looking for an organic potting mix for use in growing vegetables in containers," and they will set you up fine. Or, as we'll discuss here, you can make your own if you are feeling crafty.

Buying the potting soil from the store will ensure that you have exactly what your plants crave but it can end up costing you a pretty penny. Making your own will save you this penny and it really isn't that hard. An excellent homemade soil is composed of a growing medium, a material to keep in moisture, and another to allow for the plant to be drained.

Before we get started at making our own soil, it is important to consider fertilizing that soil. When you buy a pre-made mix from the store, it will start out with plenty of nutrients. However, your plants are going to suck up those nutrients so that they can grow. Since your plants continue to need these nutrients, adding fertilizer to the soil is done in order to keep it. If you choose to make your own potting mix then you should also add a little bit of fertilizer at the beginning and then, same with the pre-bought mix, add more to it on a regular schedule. A couple of ways of adding fertilizer are to add some limestone to your homemade soil at the beginning and to top-dress the plants with healthy compost, such as mushroom compost. Of course, there are also many kinds of fertilizer that you can find at your local garden store. Now let's take a look at those recipes.

If you want to create a potting soil that is designed to function the same way that store- bought potting soil does, then you want to take a large pot and add in your three ingredients. For a growing medium you can use the kind of garden soil you would find at any hardware store. These mediums should already be treated to ensure that they are free of disease or weeds. Of course, you could always just go out and scoop up some soil yourself, but this is almost certainly guaranteed to be a bad idea. In order to ensure that moisture, and therefore more nutrients, are retained in your mix, you should add in peat moss. Finally, you want to make sure your mix won't drown your plants, and this means adding a drainage material such as vermiculite, sand, or perlite. Take these three ingredients and mix them, keeping the proportions equal. You want your potting mix to be loose when you stir but to clump up when you squeeze it in your hands.

For some people, this mix is not organic enough. Another recipe for homemade potting mix, this time favored by organic growers, is to mix garden soil and compost. You can actually go to the store and purchase compost for this reason, or you can make your own. The best compost for growing vegetables comes from a mixture of vegetable scraps or peelings, bread, eggshells, pieces of fruit, or coffee grounds. Whatever you do, make sure you don't include any animal products like meat or fat or even daily products. You want the compost to be half green, half brown (such as using dried leaves or scraps of cardboard). Mix one-half soil, one-half compost, and add sand to the mix to allow for drainage.

Whether you use store-bought or you make your own, it's important to give your plants what they need.

Lights, Fans, Humidifiers

INDOOR GARDENING

We talked about the need for lights, fans, and humidifiers in the last chapter, so we will only briefly touch on them here so that you can add them to your shopping list as needed. As with everything, there is quite a range of prices that you can find yourself paying for this equipment. Truthfully, though, don't think that more money equals better plants. It is almost always a smarter choice to start small and get the more expensive gear down the road as you better understand what you are doing.

Fans and humidifiers are very easy to understand. You want a humidifier that will give you the 40-50% levels you need, and you want a fan that will blow air. This means pretty much any humidifier or fan will do the trick. Now, if you want to get a little fancier, you can purchase models that regulate themselves. A humidifier that knows when to turn off and on by reading the room can save you having to finetune the schedule of garden maintenance. However, this can still be done with cheaper models by purchasing a timer. By using a timer, you can set your cheap fan or humidifier to turn off and on based on the schedule you built using the information you collected in the previous chapter. You can also use a timer for your grow lights, which we'll turn our attention to now.

Although the lights in your home might make the room plenty bright for you, your plants are far more discriminating when it comes to the light they crave.

INDOOR GARDENING

Plants use light to go through a process called photosynthesis, and the lights in your home just won't do the trick to trigger this. That means purchasing lights especially designed for plants. What separates regular lights from plant lights is the spectrum of light that they produce. Go to a site like Amazon and open up the product page for the first light you can find. You'll notice that the description includes numbers with a K afterward such as 3000K. This tells you how warm or how cold the light is. The higher the number, the colder the light. While there are quite a few plants that will grow with a cold light, if you want a proper and healthy harvest, then you will need a warmer light in the 3000K range. There are three primary kinds of lights that growers purchase for their indoor gardens. Feel free to choose the kind that is right for you, but just make sure that it is a warm light so that your plants are happy with it, and you don't need to replace it for a warmer one down the road.

Fluorescent grow lights are used quite regularly by indoor growers. The standard bulb, referred to as the T12, is often used to help provide extra light for plants near windows. However, the T12 is not overly strong, and so these lights need to be placed close to the plants in order to really provide any benefit. More appropriate for an indoor gardener is the T5 bulb. Thinner than the T12, the T5 is a more powerful light that is strong enough to care for a plant without the extra boost of natural sunlight. If you are going to go with fluorescent

INDOOR GARDENING

grow lights, then you are best served by purchasing a T5 or a similarly powerful variation thereof.

LED grow lights have become very popular lately. These lights are more expensive than the fluorescent ones, but they are designed to use only half as much electricity. This means that purchasing an LED grow light might cost you up-front, but it will save you money in the long run. They also last four to five times longer than fluorescent bulbs do, which makes those savings even more impressive. Keep in mind that if you are looking to use an LED light for your garden, then you are going to need to purchase one specifically meant for use with plants because most LED lights are simply not strong enough. But those that have been intended for plants are typically far more intense than the fluorescent bulbs are. LED lights also don't run as hot, which means that they won't make as large of an impact on your grow space's overall temperature.

HID grow lights were the most popular light for indoor gardeners before the rise of LED technology. People who were only raising one or two plants would go with fluorescent bulbs while those with many would always turn to HID. They are the most expensive of the three kinds but they also tend to be the most powerful. They don't use electricity sparingly either, so they can lead to a heavier electricity bill compared to the other kinds of light. However, they are great for growing plants like tomatoes that have a lot of foliage because the intensity allows the light to get through to the roots easier. HID lights come in high pressure sodium and metal halide varieties. High pressure sodium lights are used for the flowering phase of the plant's life, while metal halide is used during the vegetative growth period. You can get away with using just one of these types throughout the whole growth cycle, but if you decide to use both for your indoor garden, then you will need to buy two different types of fixtures rather than just swap out the bulbs between a single fixture.

While the choice of what type of light to use is entirely your own, it is this author's recommendation that you begin with a decent LED grow light. As the middle option, they will still cost more to set up than a fluorescent light does, but the longer life cycle and the reduced electricity consumption will quickly make up for this investment. LED grow lights will also allow you to produce more plants at the same time than the fluorescent bulbs will. Before you add the lights to your shopping list, let's first consider how much illumination you will need to provide.

As a rule of thumb, if you are growing a plant that produces any type of food, then it is pretty safe to assume that it will require a minimum of 30 watts of light for every square foot. However, because we are looking not just to keep the plants alive but to produce an amazing harvest, the best bet is to aim to provide 50 watts per square foot instead. To figure out how much you require, you will need a measuring tape. Measure out the grow space that you have set aside for your plants. Multiply the length by the width to get the square footage. Take this number and multiply it by 50, which is to say multiply the square footage of your grow area by the amount of wattage your plants need. This gives you the exact wattage that you need to purchase. Every light that you can buy will have the wattage listed on the package or, if you are buying online, the store page. Divide the total wattage you need by how many watts the light puts out. This number tells you exactly how many lights you need. Here's an example of the math:

A 5x5 grow area has a square footage of 25. 25 multiplied by 50 equals 1250, which means that this grow area requires 1250 watts of light. The first grow light I found shows a wattage of 185, so I will take 1250 and divide it by 185 to get 6.75. Round this up to 7. I now know exactly how many lights I need to purchase. Keep in mind, this example is using a made-up space and the first grow light I found on a quick Google search. Your space and the lights you purchase may line up to these numbers, but it is more likely that you will need to calculate your specific numbers. Once you have, you know exactly how many lights to provide for your plants and can add these to your shopping list.

Everything Else You Need

INDOOR GARDENING

Even when the big equipment has all been tackled, there will still be quite a few pieces that you will want to purchase before you start your garden. These range from hand tools to oils and soil test kits. The good news is that most of these will only cost you a couple of dollars each and can be found in pretty much any gardening or hardware store. But first, we won't be covering seeds here. If you want to grow a plant, you will need to purchase seeds or a young plant. This one should go without saying and only you know exactly what fruits and vegetables you are interested in growing. If you don't yet know, we'll be covering fruits, vegetables, and herbs in chapters four, five and six.

As your plants grow, you will find yourself needing to take care of them, and maintaining their health will mean tools. But if you want your plants to grow at all, you will need to water them. You have three options for this. The first is to get yourself a watering can and use that. While using a watering can simply makes it easier to pour the water, many people enjoy using them because they give the feeling of being a "real" gardener. You can just as easily save your money and use a measuring cup or even a simple drinking cup. Just remember to keep the gardening cup separate from those you drink from as there are times when you will want to add plant nutrients to your water that you wouldn't care to directly consume yourself! Finally, if you are looking for a more expensive but mostly hands-free approach, you can always purchase a system that automates your watering for you on a timer.

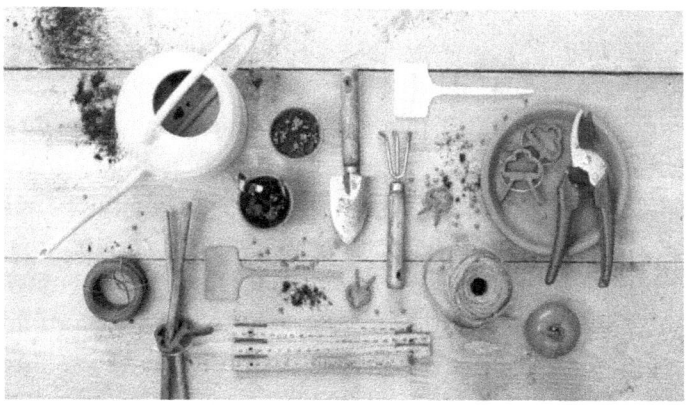

In order to trim and maintain the plants as they grow, you will want to get several types of hand tools. First up is a set of shears for pruning. You'll need to cut your plants at certain points to promote healthy growth or to remove infected limbs. You could use a set of scissors, but these may create a harsh cut, which would hurt your plant. Every time you cut your plants, they receive a shock to their system. A good set of shears will ensure that the cuts you do make as little harm as possible. You will also want to get a small rake for the soil and a trowel, though these aren't nearly as important as shears. What is as important is to get yourself a spade. You'll want to be able to dig down underneath the roots, especially when they are young, and you need to move them from their seeding pot to the larger growing pot.

While you will more than likely find yourself using shears to remove unhealthy limbs, the best option available to us gardeners is to prevent infection or infestation before it happens. We already spoke about some ways of doing this earlier, but another effective way is to purchase some neem oil. Neem oil is made out of natural chemicals found from pressing vegetable oil out of the fruit and seeds of the neem herb. These chemicals are used to deter pests like mites and to strive off infectious diseases and fungi. You can purchase it at pretty much any gardening center, and it should be applied to your plants once every week. Since it is most cost-efficient to purchase neem oil in pour bottles, you will also want to get a spray bottle from your local dollar store. This is one of those purchases that many indoor gardeners assume they won't need, but they quickly regret not investing in neem oil when they lose their fruits and veggies to a preventable cause like fungi.

Although you will want to have a thermometer for reading the temperature of your grow space, you will also want a soil thermometer to get a crystal-clear sense of how your plants are doing. You can always get one and use it to test the soil of your various pots from time to time. However, most are cheap enough that it makes more sense just to purchase one for each container, and leave it in place so that you can always check the soil temperature at a glance. Speaking of the soil, it is a good idea to get a test kit so that you can check the pH level of your pots. The pH level basically gives you an understanding of the nutrients and the chemical balance of the soil. Most plants want it to be between 5.5 to 7.5, with the majority right around the middle of that range. Test kits tend to come with several uses but run out quickly. Many gardeners will want to invest in an electronic pH reader to save money and time in the long run.

Once you have these tools, you will have all of the essentials necessary to bring your first plants from seed to harvest. As you grow accustomed to working with your indoor garden, you are likely to discover new tools that will make your life easier, but these can be purchased as the need arises.

INDOOR GARDENING

Chapter Summary

- Starting a new garden means getting your hands on a lot of gear, but each piece has a purpose and will make your life a lot less stressful. It will ensure that your plants produce the largest harvest possible.

- Different plants require different sized containers. You will most likely want to purchase a couple of 10 or 14-inch containers for seeding your vegetables.

- The chances are that if you are looking to grow the more traditional vegetables such as cucumbers, peppers, eggplants, tomatoes, or broccoli, then you will be using either an 18 or 24-inch pot.

- You should only need a 30-inch pot if you are growing large plants like rhubarb or pumpkins. Keep in mind that these larger plants weigh more, and so the material of your 30-inch pot needs to be durable enough to support them.

- Pots come in all sorts of designs that can end up costing a lot, but your plants won't grow any better in an expensive pot than they would in a cheap one. Just make sure that whatever container you use has drainage holes.

- Many growers like wooden pots, but given that they slowly break down and the way that water

INDOOR GARDENING

can damage them, it is better to go with plastic, ceramic, or terracotta.

- Ceramic pots are heavy and expensive but quite durable. Terracotta is cheaper than ceramic and also quite durable, but they tend to dry out quicker than other types.

- Plastic pots are the cheapest and break rather easily, but they are the ones most growers go to for their light weight and affordability.

- If you want the best taking fruits and vegetables, then you really should use an organic potting mix. You can find pre-made ones at any garden store.

- A good potting soil is made up of three parts: a growing medium, a material for retaining moisture, and another to allow draining.

- You can make your homemade potting soil by combining equal parts garden soil (for growing), peat moss (moisture retention), and either sand, perlite, or vermiculite (drainage).

- You can also make an effective potting soil by combining equal parts garden soil and compost. Just make sure the compost is made out of vegetable scraps, bread, eggshells, cardboard, and fruit scraps. Avoid animal products in your garden compost as this attracts disease and hungry critters. Add sand to this mixture so it can drain.

INDOOR GARDENING

- Plants suck nutrients out of the soil, so you will want to add fertilizer over time. You can always purchase fertilizer at the store, or you can top dress your plants with your compost mix.

- While it is necessary to have a fan for airflow and a humidifier to keep your grow space at 40%-50%, these don't need to be top of the line or overly expensive models. You can always use a timer to control when they turn off and on.

- Light comes in warm and cold temperatures. The higher the K number, the colder the light. Your garden will want light in the 3000K range.

- Fluorescent grow lights are fine for one or two plants. HID grow lights are good for several plants but they're also expensive and consume a lot of power. LED lights are the best choice for those that want to save money because they last longer and take up less electricity.

- Provide your plants with 50 watts of light per square foot. Multiply the square footage of your garden by 50 to find the total number of watts you will require.

- You will want to purchase a watering can, garden shears, a small rake, a spade, and a trowel. A spray bottle and some neem oil is an absolute must. You should also get some soil thermometers and either a pH test kit or an electronic pH reader.

INDOOR GARDENING

In the next chapter, you will learn all about the operating cycle of your indoor vegetable or fruit garden. From seeding to watering and fertilizing, you will learn exactly what goes into maintaining your garden and keeping it healthy from seed to harvest.

CHAPTER THREE

THE OPERATION CYCLE OF AN INDOOR GARDEN

Now that you have everything that you need for your garden, it is time to put everything together and get your hands dirty! Since the most common way that gardeners start out is by planting seeds, we will begin with a look at how to raise our fruits and veggies from seed to seedling and then transplant them from the seeding container to the containers you have set out for your garden proper. From there, we will move onto the rest of the operation cycle, such aspects as watering and fertilizing your plants.

With the knowledge in this chapter, you will know what goes into raising your plants. Then the next three chapters will look at fruits, vegetables, and herbs, respectively. These chapters will each focus on the type of plant in question and go into specifics about them there. However, all of the plants looked at in the following chapters are raised properly by following the operation cycle laid out in this chapter.

Soiling Your Pots to Seed Your Garden

In the last chapter, we saw two ways to make our own potting soil. Of course, you can always go to your local gardening center and purchase pre-made potting soil as well, the choice of which to use is entirely yours. Regardless of which you go with, however, you are going to do pretty much the same thing with it. Fill up the containers that are to be a part of your garden so that the soil is a quarter of an inch from the rim of the pot. Since we are beginning with seeds, it is okay to only worry about filling up the smallest pots that will be used for the seedlings at this stage. Just remember that your seedlings will be moved into larger pots when they are large enough, keep an eye on their growth and add potting mix to your larger containers a day or two ahead of time so that you have everything ready for the transplanting when it is time.

Now that your pots have soil, it is time to turn your attention to the seeds that you want to plant. Assuming that you have already purchased the seeds you want from your local garden center, you could just pop them into your containers and call it a day. But it is always a better idea to help your seeds through the germination process through a little extra work. This is especially true if you are planting seeds with a hard shell such as sweet peas or spinach. You can help your plants to germinate by using one of the following three methods.

The first approach is the use of scarification. In order to help the hard shell of the seed break down properly, take the garden shears you have purchased and scrape the shell with them. You don't want to create any deep scratches that expose the inside of the shell because this can ruin the seed, you only want to slightly damage the outside to make it a little weaker. Another way to do this is to take some sandpaper and gently rub the seed to thin out the shell. If you go with the scarification approach, then you will want to plant these seeds as soon as you finish.

Stratification offers another approach that can help with hard-shelled seeds, though it is more often used for plants outside of the fruit, vegetable, or herb varieties. However, some plants such as lettuce or perennial sweet peas benefit greatly from stratification. These seeds tend to have chemicals present, which makes germination difficult or even impossible. In order to get through their hard shell, you need to use a combination of cold and warm temperatures. The best way to achieve this is by letting the seeds first soak for 24 hours in water. At the end of the soaking period, remove the seeds and put them into a sealable plastic bag with some peat moss or vermiculite and then stick them into a refrigerator. It is a good idea to cut tiny holes in the container to allow some airflow as a lack of airflow promotes mold growth. While the length of time and temperatures that seeds require for this process varies depending on the kind of plant, it typically takes two or three months before they are ready to plant.

The third method is the easiest, and that is to soak the seeds. Seeds that benefit from soaking are those with hard coats like asparagus, carrots, corn, peas, pumpkins, or squash, to name but a few. While these seeds may still grow without the soaking process, it could take them days or weeks to germinate this way. To soak your seeds, simply place them in some lukewarm water for between 12 to 24 hours. When you return to your seeds, you may notice that some of them are now floating. These can be thrown away as they are unlikely to germinate properly. Those that are still sitting peacefully at the bottom of the water will be the ones you plant. Remove your seeds and rinse them off with clean water. We do this to remove any chemicals that were released during the soaking process. Plant these seeds as soon as you finish rinsing them.

Now that you either have soft-shelled seeds ready to plant, or hard-shelled seeds that have been correctly prepared, it is time to sow them into their containers. Create a little hole for your seeds that is between a quarter to half an inch deep. You can have more than one hole in a container so long as there is enough space to keep them about an inch apart. Drop a couple of seeds into each of the holes you have made and then cover them up with soil. You don't want the covering soil to be too tightly packed, as this will make it harder for oxygen to get to the seeds and this can cause your plants to suffocate. You also don't want to make the holes too deep. Otherwise the seedlings may be unable to break out through the top. When a seed germinates, the shell breaks down, and the seedling uses this for energy to dig its way out of the soil. If it is too deep, then they won't have enough vitality to break out. You may want to cover the container with some plastic wrap in order to keep the moisture and humidity levels up. Keep these containers in a warm area, as seeds tend to require more heat than older plants do.

Even though it may be somewhat tedious at this stage, it is in your best interests to keep an eye on your plants every day. Most of the time, there won't be anything to see, just a container with some dirt in it. But before too long, you will notice a tiny stem sticking out of the earth. That stem will then start to grow branches and leaves. Once you spot these leaves, it will be time to transfer the plant to a larger container. We do this because the root system of the plant will run out of room to continue growing in these small containers and that will stunt the growth and even possibly kill the plant.

To transfer your plants to the new container, the first step is to decide which plants will be moved. Because you planted several seeds in these early pots, you will want to ensure that you transplant the strongest of the seedlings. Look to see which plant is growing the most - this will be the one that you want to transfer. You will want to transfer about one plant per container used. So if you made three holes in your containers and dropped the seeds in all three, you will move the strongest of the three and leave the other two behind. Put your hand over the bowl and spread your fingers so that your seedling sticks out between two fingers. Slowly rotate the pot so that the soil starts to fall out but the plant rests against your hand. You want to let the roots of the plant fall out into your hand. Half fill the new container with the same potting soil (always use the same; otherwise the sudden switch will shock the plant), place the plant in and add more soil. You will want the root ball to be only an inch or two from the top of the container; this is done so that there is plenty of space for the roots to continue to grow. If you already have a bowl filled with soil, then you just need to dig out a big enough hole to place the plant in. Add more soil on top of the plant so as to keep it at roughly the same depth that it had been in the first container.

If everything has gone well, then you won't see any issues and your plants will continue their growth unimpeded. Continue checking on them every day and provide the seedlings with the temperature, pH level, humidity, and water that the species needs to grow. When you do this, you will have full-grown plants in no time.

Watering Your Plants

While it is one of the most vital parts of tending for any garden, watering your indoor garden is actually a very easy process. But, since you are growing fruit and vegetables, it is worthwhile to keep in mind that watering is even more important than if you were growing flowers. This is because when they are left to go dry, vegetable plants will produce a weak harvest and may even actually ruin the entire harvest. So, if there is one part of the operation cycle that you absolutely cannot ignore, it is ensuring that your plants are correctly watered. But this isn't an excuse to drown your plants by overwatering them either; you need to be mindful of *when* you water them.

INDOOR GARDENING

Your plants are going to need to be watered frequently, far more often than the same type of plant would require if it was grown in the outdoor earth. This is because potting soil has a tendency to dry out a lot quicker than the soil in your backyard. You will also need to be mindful of the temperature; on days in which the temperature rises, you will need to water more (sometimes even multiple times in a single day). If you are unsure whether or not it is time to water your plants, there are two ways that you can see if they are ready. The first is to simply put your finger into the soil. You should stick your finger deep enough that you submerge the middle phalanx joint in the earth; this is the main joint in your finger after the knuckle. If the soil is dry, then you will want to water. The other way to check is to lift the container or tip it slightly onto its side. Try doing this when you first water the plants and then later to monitor them. You will notice that the container is much lighter when it is dry, so this simple weight check lets you know if it is time to water.

It is necessary to ensure that you thoroughly water your plants. When potting soil is dry, it can actually be a bit of a pain to effectively water it. The root ball will sometimes move away from the sides of the container when it is dry, and this creates a situation that when you water the plant, all of the water goes down the sides of the container in the divots that the roots leave behind. You can get around this issue by always watering your plants so that the water level rises to the top of the container. Doing this guarantees the roots of your plant get plenty of water. However, this can easily lead to drowning the plant, so it is worth checking the soil first to make sure it is the right time to water.

Keep in mind that there is a difference between dry soil and moist soil. When you remove your finger from the potting mix, moist soil will stick to it. If this happens, then it isn't yet time to water. While vegetable plants should never be left to dry out, it's an excellent idea to always read the instructions that come with the seeds, as well as asking an employee at your local gardening center. Browse reliable Internet sites for the best care practices for that species. Different plants have different water needs, so always inform yourself about the needs of your plant first rather than just assume what is best for them.

INDOOR GARDENING

Fertilizing Your Indoor Garden

Human beings need to drink and eat. When we consider watering, it is clear that plants also need to drink lots of fluids. But as it so happens, plants also need to eat. Only they need their nutrients to come from the soil or a liquid fertilizer. The roots of your plants stretch out underneath the soil, spreading in order to seek out more food to provide all the nutrients that they need to keep growing nice and healthy. If you are raising your plants in the ground outdoors, then those roots can stretch a good distance and find lots of nutrients. But when you raise those same plants indoors, there is only so much space in each container that they can spread out, and there are only so many nutrients in the soil. To make certain your indoor plants eat their fill, you need to fertilize them on a regular basis.

Regardless of what potting soil you decide to use, your plants will suck it dry of nutrients in less than two months. When this happens, they will begin to starve. You can buy time in this process by adding a slow-release fertilizer or manure pellets (such as chicken) into the soil. However, these are only going to buy your plants a certain amount of breathing space. They won't be enough on their own to keep your plants from starving. For that, you are going to need to create a schedule to regularly feed your plants a liquid fertilizer. There are many liquid fertilizers available on the market that you can purchase, or you can make your own. We'll see how to make our own in a moment, but before we do, it is a good idea to understand what exactly a fertilizer is providing for your plants. By gaining a knowledge of this, you have the best possible understanding of what they require.

The majority of fertilizers available are primarily focused on providing three nutrients to your plants: nitrogen, phosphorus, and potassium, or NPK. I say the majority of fertilizers because there are a decent amount on the market those focuses on only one of these three nutrients rather than all three. You can also purchase these nutrients on their own in a solid form meant to be dissolved in water. However, if you are purchasing pre-made fertilizer for your indoor garden, then the best idea

INDOOR GARDENING

is to choose a fertilizer that has an NPK ratio with equal amounts of each nutrient. Of course, it is rare that it is always a one for one ratio, and so it is okay for the ratio to be a little uneven so long as the nutrients are present in approximately equal quantities. If you are growing fruit or plants that fruit such as strawberries, raspberries, tomatoes, or peppers, then you are going to want to use a fertilizer with a higher amount of potassium as this helps the plants to grow their fruits properly. When using a store-bought fertilizer, you should always follow the instructions on the package so that you avoid overfeeding. When you overfeed them, the pH level in the soil rises to high levels. If you bought soil testing kits or an electronic pH reader, then you should keep a close eye on the pH level.

Buying fertilizer can quickly become expensive if you have a large garden to maintain. One way around this rising cost is to make your own. But be aware that it is always a very smelly process! One way to quickly get yourself some fertilizer is to fill a bag up with compost and let it soak in water for ten days. On day ten, you add water to the mixture until the color changes from black to slightly gray like tea, at which point it is ready to use. Another simple fertilizer uses urine as the primary ingredient since it is sterile, has a decent amount of potassium, and a lot of nitrogen in it, plus it's very easy to acquire because you can use your own! Dilute one part urine with forty parts water, and you have yourself a quick and efficient fertilizer. However, although this method is a little more difficult, you may be interested in making a comfrey fertilizer due to its high potassium concentration. The same steps you take to make a comfrey fertilizer can be used to make a nettle or a borage fertilizer if you need a higher nitrogen count.

Comfrey is a herb from Europe that has high levels of potassium, phosphorus, and nitrogen. That means this one herb can provide you with all the NPK you need from a fertilizer. There are ways to turn this into a fine fertilizer, but it's necessary to note that what is really great about comfrey is that you can grow it yourself as a part of your herb garden so that you can always have plenty of source material to turn into fertilizer. It is pretty much one of the best investments you can make when it comes to feeding your plants. When there is too much carbon in a plant bed, this can make it hard for the plants to get the best benefits from the nitrogen in the soil. Comfrey has a carbon-nitrogen ratio that is perfect in preventing any of these issues.

To make fertilizer out of comfrey, all you need to do is stuff a bunch of comfrey leaves into a large container. Cut a little hole in the bottom of the container, and put a smaller bowl underneath to catch the black liquid that drips out. It takes a few weeks to start producing this black liquid, though it can be sped up by using a heavy object to press down on the leaves. This liquid is excellent for fertilizer when you mix it with water in a 15:1 ratio. That's all it takes to make comfrey fertilizer, but there is more you can do with comfrey around your garden. Take the leaves out after the pressing and use them to feed your potatoes or tomatoes as a nutritious mulch. As long as you let comfrey leaves wilt for a few days first, it can be used in this manner. You can also add comfrey leaves to the containers you are planning to use next to add more nutrients to the initial soil. Make sure you are using it with slightly older plants and not young seedlings as it can be too strong for them and lead to nutrient burn. Finally, you can add comfrey leaves to your compost to help make it more nutritious.

If you purchased your fertilizer, then it will have instructions on how often to use it, and you should always listen to these instructions. However, if you have created your own, then you are going to need to educate yourself on the needs of the particular plants you are looking to feed. Some, such as fruiting veggies like tomatoes or peppers, will benefit from a weekly feeding schedule. However, there are others, such as lettuce, which don't need a regular fertilizer feed. You should always research your plants before seeding them by either Googling the information or asking your local garden center employees. Also, you shouldn't try to give fertilizer to plants that are overly stressed out. While it may seem like a good idea to dose them with fertilizer to help them get better, it is actually much less stressful on the plant to be given clean water instead. You also won't need to use liquid fertilizer on your herbs, as they generally grow best by being light on nutrients.

INDOOR GARDENING

INDOOR GARDENING

Chapter Summary

- Start your seeds first in a smaller receptacle, filling the bowl up with soil so that it is a quarter of an inch from the top.

- Soft-shelled seeds can simply be placed into a hole and covered with earth, but hard- shelled seeds need to either go through scarification, stratification or soaking to weaken their shells enough for germination to happen.

- Scarification is done by gently scraping the outer layer of the seeds or by using a coarse sandpaper to file them down. It is important not to go so hard as to expose the inside of the seed. If this happens then the seed is ruined.

- Stratification is a two-step process of first soaking seeds for 24 hours and then storing them in a refrigerator. Put seeds in a sealable bag filled with peat moss or vermiculite and stick them in the fridge for two or three months until they begin to germinate, at which point you plant them in a container.

- Soaking is the easiest method as all you need to do is leave your seeds in water for 12 to 24 hours. Remove any seeds that have floated to the top, as these are no longer viable, and plants those that have remained on the bottom.

- When planting seeds, drop a couple into each hole you make for them. Even those that have passed the soaking test may not germinate properly. Plant multiple seeds and then transplant those that seem to have most vitality into bigger pots once they are large enough.

- Fruits and vegetables need plenty of water to grow properly, but too much will drown the plants. The best way to tell if a plant is ready to be watered is by performing the finger test: simply stick your finger an inch or two into the soil to see if the top inch (sometimes top two inches depending on the needs of the plant) is dry. A dry top inch means it is time to water.

- Roots will often spread out to the sides of a bowl but then shrink back into the middle when the plant is too dry. This leaves holes along the side of the containers that water can run through, which leaves your plants thirsty despite having just been watered. Because of this, always make sure that you thoroughly water the plants each and every time you do.

- To tell the difference between dry soil and moist soil, use the finger test, and see if any soil sticks to your finger when it is removed. If the soil sticks, then it is moist, not dry.

- Plants need to drink plenty of water to grow but they also need to eat plenty of nutrients. Specifically, they really need nitrogen, phosphorus, and potassium (NPK). The best fertilizers are liquid fertilizers that use natural ingredients to create an even balance between these three nutrients.

- Adding manure pellets or compost to your soil is one way to naturally increase the amount of nutrients present. Just remember to keep a close eye on the pH level of your soil, as too much will lead to nutrient burn and damage your plants.

- Store-bought fertilizers can cost a lot of money, but it is easy to make your own. One approach is to leave a bag of compost to soak in water for ten days and then add more water until the mix is a light gray color. Another approach is to mix one part urine with forty parts water.

- The absolute best fertilizer that you can make yourself comes from seeping the liquid from comfrey herb and mixing this liquid in a ratio of one part comfrey juice to 15 parts water. Comfrey leaves also work well when they're mixed into compost or fed to your plants in the form of mulch.

- Some plants like to be fertilized on a weekly basis, such as tomatoes or peppers, while others require far less, such as lettuce.

In the next chapter, you will learn what it takes to grow fruit inside your home. We'll look at why organic fruit is so highly regarded, and we'll go over how to produce your own strawberries, oranges, peaches and more.

INDOOR GARDENING

You'll love how you can have your favorite fruits without the hassle of going to the store.

CHAPTER FOUR

GROWING BEAUTIFUL FRUITS

Everything you need to know about maintaining your garden has been covered already, so now it is time to finally get into the plants themselves. Up first are the fruits, the tastiest plants of all. You'll learn what it takes to grow healthy fruit plants with large yields. There isn't enough room in this book to cover every type of fruit, so we'll stick to some of the most popular to see exactly what goes into raising delicious strawberries, peaches and more.

Just a note: While tomatoes are technically a fruit, we'll be looking at them in the next chapter. You add tomatoes to a garden salad, not a fruit punch, after all!

Why Organic Foods are Better

Going organic has become a fashionable trend these days, with more and more people jumping aboard the organic train. But going organic is more than just a trend that will pass with time. There are numerous benefits to growing and eating such foods rather than pumping your garden (and your dinner table) full of every kind of chemical imaginable. The benefits of organic fruit and produce are most recognizable at the wider level of farming and industry movements. However, there are many benefits lower down the chain that beneficially affects the people that eat these foods. Let's take a look at these now.

The main thing that separates organic foods from the rest is the lack of chemicals. There are no harmful GMOs used when growing organic. This is great since many GMOs are used alongside other harmful chemicals in modern farming practices these days. Purchasing organic foods supports farmers that care about the long-term consequences of the food they produce, and removes money from the hands of organizations willing to jeopardize your health for profit. It also reinforces healthier soil, slows the growth of super strains, saves taxpayer money (in the form of subsidies for non-organic farmers), and it keeps harmful chemicals from seeping into the oceans. But what benefits does organic farming provide you as an indoor gardener? Strictly speaking, there are four answers to that question.

The first benefit is the taste. A stressed plant tastes bad - it is just a fact. A lot of the GMO produced crops are under a lot of stress, and you can tell the difference when you compare a GMO grown fruit to one that has been organically grown. Stressed-out plants need to spend their energy repairing themselves and searching out more nutrients. Meanwhile, a healthy organically grown plant can concentrate its strength on producing the best fruit possible. That, in turn, means juicier, larger, tastier fruits (and veggies!), and this is wonderful news for your taste buds.

Organic foods also have more nutrients and antioxidants than those grown through chemical processes. Therefore, the fruits you are growing organically in your apartment are going to be super-great for you and your health. The extra nutrients come from the soil that is employed in organic growing. We aim to use compost and natural fertilizers to keep our potting soil nutrient-rich for our fruits and vegetables, and this shows its benefits in the nutrient content of the fruits we produce. Fruit developed organically typically has 30% more antioxidants when compared to GMO grown products. That's a huge increase when you remember that organic fruit also tastes better. Not only does it taste better but it *is* better for you, period.

Growing organic food promotes a healthier lifestyle in general. It is my belief that, when you see how great the food from your indoor garden tastes, you'll agree. Many gardeners enjoy sharing their harvest with friends and family and this, in turn, spreads the joys of organic farming to more people. Once people have experienced how much more delicious your fruits are, they are that much more likely to reach for the organically grown produce next time they are shopping. That means more money flowing into healthy farming practices that promote wellness. Plus, when you are growing your own fruit, you can't help but become that much more involved in what you put in your body, and this leads to people making healthier choices regarding their wellbeing and fitness.

Finally, growing organic fruits and vegetables will teach you about how much further products can go. Most people toss out their compost and never spend even a second thinking about how it could be used. Once you start saving your compost for your crops and studying the ways you can make use of your plants (such as the many benefits of comfrey), you will realize there are many more uses for the goods around you than you ever previously imagined. These factors promote a lifestyle that is more sustainable and gets as much use out of the stuff around you as is possible. While this may seem an odd reason to favor organic fruit, this subtle shift in perspective is bound to have a major impact on your carbon footprint and the way you consider waste.

Growing Gorgeous Strawberries

Strawberries are a favorite of indoor gardeners and not just because of their delicious taste. Rather, they are a favorite because they are easy to grow almost anywhere, whether that is sitting on your windowsill, or set into a vertical growing setup along a wall. They aren't particularly large plants, which makes them quite versatile. While they are best grown at a temperature between 68F or 77F, they can grow at both warmer or colder temperatures as well. You should note, while they can tolerate temperatures outside of the normal, what they can't tolerate are sudden changes in the temperature. When strawberry plants are forced to experience drastic temperature drops, they can get stressed to the point of damage, and they will produce a dramatically reduced yield when it comes time to harvest. Strawberries are able to grow in the shade but they much prefer to have direct light.

The unique thing about growing strawberries indoors is that you actually have to pollinate them yourselves. When growing outdoors, the best way to pollinate strawberry plants is by using honey bees. However, this is clearly not an option indoors! But the pollination still has to happen or you won't get any berries. So, in order to ensure a good harvest, you need to pollinate your strawberries by hand. You will know that your plants are ready to be pollinated when the petals of the strawberry flowers open up completely. Strawberry plants have gendered parts with a greenish-yellow female part (the pistil) and a brown male part (the stamen). The procedure to follow is as follows: take a small brush, like those used for makeup, and brush the pollen from the stamen down into the pistil. Do this for each and every flower on the plant. You want to make sure that the entire pistil is covered, otherwise you will end up with misshapen and deformed berries that are rather unappealing. Many gardeners go over each flower twice so that they can be super-sure that everything has been correctly pollinated. You can pollinate the flowers every day if you want (and many people do). When the white petals of the flower start to die off and leave green leaves (called sepal), then you know the pollination was successful, and you will soon have strawberries growing.

When it comes to watering strawberry plants, how much they require depends on what part of the growth cycle they've reached. In the early stages, they need far less water and typically can go a few days without watering. However, they will need to be watered on a daily basis during the fruiting phase of their life cycle, otherwise they get too dry and produce a poor yield. While watering the plants, keep in mind the pH level of the soil. Strawberries like to have a pH level in the 6.0 to 6.5 range, but they can tolerate a 0.5 difference either way. They use nitrogen to produce healthy leaves, and phosphorous and potassium are used to flower and produce berries. Be careful about the amount of nitrogen your strawberries are receiving; too much will cause the leaves to grow large, but this comes at the cost of fewer flowers, and the berries themselves will be much more susceptible to disease.

Strawberries are prone to the same pests and diseases that most plants have to deal with, and they also attract animals like rats or mice. Birds also love to eat strawberries, but this shouldn't be a problem so long as your windows are closed! Pets are also prone to either eat the berries or dig in the soil. Be mindful of these threats and keep an eye out for giveaway signs such as paw marks in the soil or partially eaten berries or leaves. As long as the berries are kept safe from pests and critters, they can be plucked off the plant and eaten immediately. You will know they are ripe and ready when they reach a beautiful and bold red color.

Growing an Indoor Peach Tree

It may come as a surprise to learn that peach trees actually thrive when grown indoors. While the species grown for peach farming is far too large to fit into most houses, there is such a thing as dwarf peach trees which don't take up nearly as much space. Despite being a smaller variety, these dwarf peach trees have a large enough yield to make it well worth the effort it takes to grow. A dwarf tree, so long as it is properly pruned, can be kept around five feet. Besides pruning, you'll find they are surprisingly easy to take care of.

When picking out a peach tree species to grow, you don't have to worry too much about their preferred climate since you will be raising it indoors. If it is growing in the same location as the rest of your fruits and vegetables, then climate is a concern; otherwise, you can use equipment to provide a perfect growing space for your tree. What is most important is the size of the species of peach tree and whether or not it self-pollinates. Some dwarf species which make for great plants are the golden glory, honey babe, or peregrine trees. Bonsai peach trees also come in manageable sizes, and the autumn red species is particularly delicious.

Once you know what kind of peach tree you want to grow, you then need to decide if you'd like to grow it from a pit or if you want to purchase a young tree. A young tree may be ready for harvest in a year or so, but growing from a pit will take a minimum of three years before your tree starts to grow peaches. If you do decide to grow from a pit, then you will first want to test your pit to ensure it can actually grow. To do this, you just need to drop the pit into a bowl of water and see if it sinks. Just like when hard-shelled seeds float up to the top during soaking, if your peach pit floats, then it is no good. Once your pit passes the sinking test, you should use the stratification method to prepare the seed. Remember, it is always a good idea to prepare more than one pit at a time because even pits that pass the sinking test may not germinate in the right way once they have been planted. You will know that the pits are ready to be planted when they begin to grow roots.

INDOOR GARDENING

While the seedling may seem a little small, you'll want to transplant it to a five gallon pot. Most of the time that we are growing plants, we aim to provide them with a pot that gives them plenty of room to grow. Since this is a tree we are growing indoors, we can help keep the tree a manageable size by using a smaller container like this. Line the bottom of the pot with gravel to promote drainage and to give the container some more weight so that it stays in place. A light container may fall over and collapse under the weight of the tree and, not only is this bad for the health of your tree, it can also cause a major mess in your house. Fill up the rest of the container with your chosen potting mix and make sure to include some compost (especially if it has some comfrey mixed in) to

INDOOR GARDENING

impart plenty of nutrients to the soil. Dig out a little hole to drop your seeds into and gently cover them with the earth. If you waited until the roots started to grow during the stratification process, then you will see your peach tree sticking out of the soil in a few short days.

Peach trees really enjoy their light, and the more you can give them the better they will respond. You should aim to give them six or more hours of light a day. While they will continue to stay healthy with as little as four hours a day, you will notice a much smaller yield, and it will take far longer for them to grow. Most peach trees will want a temperature of 75F during the summer, and a temperature of 45F during the winter. Peach trees go dormant during the winter, and they require this reduction in temperature to maintain their health. If you keep the temperature high during their dormant period, then you are only going to damage the tree. You can't just trick your peach tree into skipping winter; you need to learn to work with the schedule that it sets for you.

How often your peach tree needs to be watered will also depend on the season. Plants grown inside need to be watered more often than those grown in the earth, and peach trees are no different in this regard. During the summer period, you can expect to water your tree every day or two. During the winter, the need for water is far less, and you can find yourself going a week or two between watering. Use the finger test to check how dry the soil is to determine whether or not it is time to water.

You will want to check the top two inches of the earth when it comes to peach trees, so put your finger in up to the knuckle. Indoor peach trees also require more fertilizer than those grown outdoors. Fertilizing should happen every other week. Use a fertilizer that is high in phosphorus. A good rule of thumb to remember is that if the fertilizer is good for tomato plants, then it is good for your peach tree. You don't need to fertilize your tree during the dormant period, only during the growing season.

You will want to prune your tree on a yearly basis. Doing this helps to keep the tree from growing too big, and it will also eventually lead to new branches that will go on to produce more delicious peaches. Wait until the buds of your tree begin to show some pink blooms and then trim. You'll find this occurs near the start of the growing period. You do not want to prune your peach tree during its dormant phase, as this is an extra stressful time for it to undergo that kind of shock. Peaches grow on young branches, those around one year in age, so you can expect to prune a good 40% of the branches away every year. Dead branches, damaged branches, or diseased branches should all be removed at this time. If you notice branches that are starting to shoot off and grow upwards, then you may want to remove these as well. When you remove those branches that are growing upwards the plant begins to focus its energy on expanding outwards instead, and so this is a good way to prevent the tree from getting too tall. If you are growing a self-pollinating tree, then you don't need to worry about the flowers at this stage. If you need to manually pollinate your tree, then you can follow the steps listed above on how to deal with strawberry plants.

You will notice a lot of little peaches beginning to grow on your plant. While this will look like a wonderful yield, you are going to want to remove some of these peaches. Wait until they are about an inch in size, and then remove any peaches that have clustered together so that there are about 4 or 5 inches between each peach. This may seem like a weird thing to do, reducing the size of your yield, but what you are doing is making it easier for the remaining peaches to get enough energy to grow big and healthy. You will find this produces bigger, juicier peaches. The peaches are ready to be harvested when they start to smell like a peach should. Give a peach a squeeze: if it is still hard, then it isn't ready, but if it squishes then it is.

Caring for Indoor Oranges

Most people don't consider the possibility of growing an orange tree indoors. Yet fruits of the citrus variety take quickly to indoor growing conditions. So long as you are able to provide your orange tree with the right environment, you will be able to produce delicious oranges inside your own home. It is especially rewarding to grow oranges indoors because of the wonderful fragrances that these plants produce. It is like having a natural air freshener in your living room.

As with peaches, you will want to choose one of the varieties of orange tree that is considered to be a dwarf offshoot of those trees that are grown outdoors. You need to live in a very specific climate to grow oranges outdoors, but thanks to modern technology, we are able to create whatever conditions our trees need when raised indoors. Some species of orange tree that grow quite well indoors are Tahitian, satsuma, or calamondin oranges. The Tahitian produces very sweet oranges that are quite small, almost a mixture of a tangerine and a lemon. The satsuma tree produces tangerines and has quite a strange fragrance. The calamondin orange tree produces a small fruit that has a tangy, sour taste. Of the three, the calamondin is the type most often grown indoors.

Orange seeds are of the hard-shell variety, but they are much easier to plant when compared to the peach tree seed. While the peach tree seed takes several months of preparation due to their need for stratification, orange tree seeds only need to undergo the soaking process. If you set your seeds to soak before you go to bed, they will be ready for planting by lunchtime the following day. Just remember to toss out any seeds that are floating on top of the water. Plant your seeds in your starting pot, ensuring that the soil mixture has plenty of vermiculite, perlite, sand, or gravel to promote drainage.

You will need to transfer the young tree into a bigger container when you start to see leaves sticking out of the soil. Some gardeners suggest repotting orange trees once every couple of years. If you notice that the soil is drying out faster than normal, start seeing the roots of the tree sticking out of the drainage holes of its container, or the leaves begin to look unhealthy, then these are all signs that it is time to transplant your tree to a different container. Pick out a larger container and wait for spring, as this is the best time to transfer the tree. Much like the peach tree, it is harmful to transplant orange trees during the offseason. To properly repot your tree, you should first wait until the soil has dried out, which should take only a day or two. Using your garden tools, carefully break the earth away from the edges of the container so that nothing is sticking to the pot. Grasp the trunk of the tree as close to the soil as you can and very carefully lift the tree out of the bowl, and place it into the new container, which should be roughly a quarter filled with soil. Add more soil over the top of the roots of the tree and then immediately water the tree. Because you had to allow the tree to dry out before moving it, it is important that you make sure it has plenty of water over the next couple of weeks and doesn't go dry again. The period after replanting your orange tree is very stressful to it, and you want to pay extra close attention to its needs during this time.

Orange trees have a complicated relationship with water. When it comes to the container they are housed in, orange trees want good drainage and plenty of aeration for the roots. They also want a bowl that can hold plenty of moisture, so containers made out of terracotta, wood, or ceramics will definitely require extra attention to ensure the trees don't dry out. The best way to figure out how regularly to water your tree is to pay attention to how rapidly the soil dries out. Each tree has a mind of its own when it comes to how quickly it uses up its water. A good habit when starting out is to perform the finger test twice a day, once in the morning and once at night. This will give you a clear picture of how quickly your tree uses water, and once you have that, you can create a schedule accordingly. When watering, always ensure the water soaks into the soil, and doesn't just dribble down the sides of the container. Keep in mind that, just like peach trees, your orange tree has different watering needs depending on the season. Orange trees require more water in spring and summer, though overwatering them is a recipe for root rot. Even when they are the thirstiest, avoid excessively watering them. They will require much less water in the fall and winter, and it is best to wait until the finger test reveals a dry top inch rather than a mostly dry one. When it comes to checking the dryness of your trees, it is all about the top inch of the soil. The roots should never be allowed to dry out, though you will probably only need to water an orange tree a few times a week when warm, and once every week or so when cold. Finally, be careful to make sure the temperature of the water is matched to the temperature of the plant. Watering an orange tree with hotter or colder water stresses out an orange tree, and that results in a poorer yield and lower quality fruit.

Since orange trees are primarily grown in tropical weather, they will want to have a higher humidity level than many of the other plants in your indoor garden. Where most garden plants prefer a humidity level between 40% and 50%, your orange tree is going to want the humidity to be between 50% and 70%. Achieving this indoors isn't always simple, and too much heat during the colder months will damage the tree. One way that you can help your orange tree to achieve this is by misting the leaves on a regular basis; this practice, when combined with the use of a humidifier, should be enough to keep your tree healthy. As far as heat is concerned, an orange tree considers 68F to be the perfect temperature. Sudden changes in the temperature will harm it, so it is best to keep it away from windows where sunlight will overheat it, or a windy draft will cool it off. That said, orange trees like a slight drop in temperature during the night, usually down somewhere between 63F or 58F.

Orange trees like to be in very bright areas, but they don't enjoy getting direct sunlight. Instead, they grow best when they receive about eight hours of indirect light a day. Just like human beings burn when we stay out in the sun too long, direct sunlight can cause burns to the leaves of an orange tree. If you are providing lighting for your trees through electronic means, then you don't need to worry as much about direct or indirect light, just so long as the grow lamps you have purchased don't run too hot. LEDs are particularly perfect for orange trees; they provide plenty of wattage without a massive amount of excess heat.

Your tree will require lots of nutrients in order to grow and fruit to its best potential. A pH level between 6.0 and 7.5 is ideal. You can expect to use a liquid fertilizer on your tree once every week during the growing season. Unlike peach trees, orange trees continue to grow all year long rather than go dormant, but they do reduce the speed of their growth during the fall and winter. The fact that they don't become inactive means that you will need to continue fertilizing them all year round. However, you should change the feeding schedule to every other week instead. Oranges are a citrus fruit like lemons or grapefruit, and these species need more micronutrients than many of the other plants in your indoor garden. It is best to purchase a citrus fertilizer that has plenty of zinc, iron, manganese, and magnesium in it. Of course, you don't want to sacrifice the NPK content of your fertilizer, either. Given that citrus requires such a specific diet, it is better to seek out a specially designed fertilizer rather than create your own.

An orange tree doesn't need to be pruned as often as a peach tree does. If you are going to prune your tree, you should wait until branches are at least four inches before removing them. You should also prune in the warmer months to control the direction of growth. In the colder months, pruning should be done to remove damaged or sick branches so as to promote a healthier tree. You will notice that during the colder months, especially at the start of the new year, your orange tree begins to lose leaves. This time of year is often hard on the tree, and it is very important to pay close attention to how many leaves it is losing. A few leaves aren't a big deal, but anything above a few is a sign that there are environmental issues that need to be addressed. If you notice that the leaves are turning yellow, then this is not an environmental issue, but rather a telltale sign that there is a nutrient deficiency that needs to be dealt with.

Finally, your orange tree will begin to flower in the colder months of the year. You will be able to tell this is happening not only by the gorgeous white blossoms that start to open up on the tree but also by the strong fragrance of citrus that they produce. When the flowers begin to bloom, it is time to get out your trusty pollinating brush and get to work. Go over each blossom twice to ensure that everything is pollinated effectively (the same as you do with strawberries). As long as you look after the environmental, watering, and nutritional needs of your orange tree and do your best to avoid causing it unnecessary stress, then you will have delicious homegrown oranges in no time.

INDOOR GARDENING

Chapter Summary

- More than being merely a fashionable trend, organic farming techniques remove harmful GMOs from our food. They also reduce the amount of poisonous chemicals seeping into our oceans, remove money from the hands of chemical farmers and puts it into the hands of those that care about natural growing, reduces the growth of super strains, saves taxpayer money and promotes healthier soil.

- For the indoor gardener, the benefits of organically grown foods are just as significant. Organically grown fruits and vegetables don't undergo as much stress as chemically grown ones do, and this allows for much tastier harvests. The number of nutrients and antioxidants in organically grown food is also much higher than those that are chemically developed. Taking the time to grow organically promotes both a healthier lifestyle and a more sustainable one too.

- Strawberries require a temperature between 68F and 77F. Just make sure that whatever temperature you pick stays consistent, or your plants can be damaged through the stress of changing.

- Strawberries need to be pollinated by hand. Take a makeup or paintbrush and brush the pollen from the stamen of the strawberry blossom into the pistil. Do this for every blossom on the plant

INDOOR GARDENING

and then go over them a second time to ensure an even spread.

- Strawberries can go a few days without water in the early stages of growth but will require daily watering when they begin to fruit. They want a soil pH at the 6.0 to 6.5 level and need extra nitrogen while vegetative, but extra potassium and phosphorus when flowering and fruiting. When fruiting, reduce their nitrogen intake, or you will end up with a smaller harvest that is more prone to disease.

- To grow a peach tree indoors, it is a good idea to choose a dwarf variety, such as the golden glory, honey babe, or peregrine. Bonsai trees, such as the autumn red, also stay within a nice size range for indoor gardeners.

- To grow from a seed, you are going to need to stratificate the seeds prior to planting. Peach seeds will take a couple of months in refrigeration before they are ready to be planted. It is a good idea to prepare several seeds at one time in case one of them doesn't properly germinate.

- Use either a heavyweight container or line the bottom of your container with gravel. Gravel will promote better drainage while also weighing the container down so the weight of the tree doesn't collapse it on you. Fill the rest of the container with potting mix and compost.

INDOOR GARDENING

- Peach trees want at least six hours of light a day, a temperature of 75F in the summer, and 45F during their dormant winter phase. Keeping the temperature high during the winter phase will damage the tree.

- Peach trees need to be watered every day or two during the summer and once every week or two during the winter. The finger test will let you know when it is time to water, just make sure to check the top two inches for peach trees.

- Fertilize your peach tree every other week during the summer. You don't need to fertilize them at all during the winter. Pruning your tree to control the direction of growth should happen at the start of the growing season while pruning to remove dead branches should take place during winter. Avoid pruning for growth during the dormant phase, as this only hurts the tree. Peaches only like to grow on new branches, so you can expect to remove 40% of the branches every year to promote the growth of new ones and create a bigger harvest.

- Cut off peaches that are clustered close together so that there are 4 to 5 inches between each peach. That allows the tree to spend its energy better and helps ensure each peach is as tasty as possible.

- Orange trees also grow very well indoors, though you will want to select a dwarf breed such as Tahitian, satsuma, or calamondin oranges. Calamondin is the variety most often chosen for indoor growing.

- Orange seeds need to be soaked overnight before planting. Any that float to the top of the water should be thrown out. After 12 hours, you should plant the seeds directly into a mixture with plenty of vermiculite, perlite, sand, or gravel to allow for good drainage.

- Young orange trees should be transferred to a larger container when you see leaves stick out of the soil. Ensure that the bowl or box you pick has plenty of drainage holes. To repot an orange tree, stop watering it for two days ahead of time so that the soil dries out. Carefully transfer the tree to the new container and water it immediately. Make certain you don't let a freshly transplanted orange tree go thirsty for the weeks immediately following the transplantation as this is a very vulnerable time for the tree.

- Orange trees like containers and soil that hold a lot of moisture, but they also prefer that moisture to drain rather quickly. They require more water in the summer and less in the winter, just be careful not to dehydrate them or to waterlog them. Perform the finger test often so that you never allow the roots of the tree to dry out. You can expect to water a few times a week in summer and once a week in the cold. Make sure the water is the same temperature as the tree's environment.

INDOOR GARDENING

- Keep the temperature of your orange tree around 68F during the day and 63F or 58F at night. Maintain humidity between 50% and 70%. Misting the leaves of the tree with fresh water can help achieve this. Be careful of sudden changes in the temperature, as this greatly stresses out orange trees.

- Orange trees want a pH level between 6.0 and 7.5, and they like to be fertilized on a weekly basis while growing. Orange trees don't go dormant, but they do slow their growth in the colder seasons, so you can expect to have to fertilize them all year round. It is best to use a fertilizer designed for citrus as orange trees require extra zinc, iron, manganese, and magnesium.

- You shouldn't prune an orange tree often. If you are planning to prune to control the direction of growth, then allow branches to reach four inches first and prune in the warmer months of the year. Pruning should only happen in the colder months to remove sick branches.

- During the colder months, you may notice leaves dropping off your orange tree. A few leaves aren't anything to worry about, but when a lot start to come off, this would suggest an environmental issue. If the leaves are turning yellow, then there is a nutrient deficiency to be addressed.

INDOOR GARDENING

- Orange trees flower during the colder months. Pollinate the flowers in the same way as you did the strawberries. You will have delicious oranges to eat in no time at all.

In the next chapter, you will learn what it takes to cultivate the most delicious organic vegetables imaginable. From tomatoes to cucumbers, eggplants to lettuce, you can grow all the vegetables necessary to get your three daily servings (and then some!).

CHAPTER FIVE

CULTIVATING DELICIOUS VEGETABLES

Although fruits, thanks to their natural sugars, are the sweetest of the plants you can grow indoors, most gardeners in our position, are primarily interested in growing vegetables, Why? Well, they're versatile, and they provide tons of nutritional value. We already saw that organically grown fruits produce more nutritious harvests; when you combine this increase in yield with the health benefits that come from eating plenty of vegetables, it's easy to see why growing your vegetables is a great choice. But not only is it healthy, it is also super fun!

The best part of growing vegetables indoors is that there is no offseason. You can have delicious tomatoes and cucumbers, even during the harshest of winters. Vegetables aren't going to grow in the ground when there is ten feet of snow covering it, but they will certainly grow in your home setup. Many of the vegetables you purchase from the grocery store during the winter are expensive, even though they may be lower quality products. With your indoor garden, you never have to be overcharged for less than perfect veggies again. So let's turn our attention to what it takes to raise indoor tomatoes (the fruit that, quite honestly, should have been born a vegetable!).

Tending Tasty Tomatoes

The first step to growing indoor tomatoes is to pick the variety you are going to raise. Just as we choose a dwarf species for a peach or orange tree, it is best to choose a smaller type of tomato such as a cherry or a plum tomato. While these tomatoes are smaller in size, the plants yield a large number of them. Their smaller size also means they have less skin overall, and so they can grow at a quicker speed than larger species. Some species of tomatoes that make a great addition to an indoor garden are pink ping pong, Siberia, micro tom, totem, red robin, or patio tomatoes. Most species of tomato take about 70 days to grow, though this can vary by 20 days on either end, depending what you choose. There are a lot of growers that try using chemical fertilizers to make their tomatoes grow faster so that they can make a quick profit off them. This non-organic approach results in tomatoes with a very bland taste, exactly the kind of thing we aim to avoid by growing organically.

Go ahead and add your potting mixture to the containers you are going to be starting your seeds in. While it isn't essential for the seed containers, you may want to include some hydrated lime in the primary growing receptacle (at a ratio of roughly one teaspoon per gallon of soil). This addition will change the pH level in the soil, so be mindful of that while mixing, but the calcium it adds to the potting mix will help to prevent blossom end rot, which could significantly damage your plants down the road. Tomato seeds don't need to be prepared prior to planting. To plant them, simply dig a little hole about a quarter of an inch down into the soil, and drop a couple of seeds in. Keep these holes at least an inch from each other if you are planning to raise multiple seedlings in the same container. You can use plastic wrap or a cover for the container to help keep the seed containers from drying out. A temperature of 80F is ideal for germination, and you can expect to notice seedlings poking out of the soil anywhere between one to two weeks from planting. You should remove the plastic wrap or cover as soon as you see your seedlings.

INDOOR GARDENING

You should transplant your tomatoes once your seedlings are roughly an inch and a half tall. Choose the healthiest seedlings from each container, and move them into a larger container throughout the vegetative and fruiting stages of their life cycle. These young seedlings are going to need lots of light from the moment they poke out of the dirt, and this will continue throughout their life. They like it bright and warm, preferring to have between 18 to 24 hours of light. While this can make them an expensive plant when it comes to the electric bill, it also makes them an easy one to look after. You can just leave a light on rather than schedule an artificial day and night schedule for them.

You will want to use a liquid fertilizer with a high nitrogen content during this vegetative stage of your tomatoes. Continue providing them with 18 to 24 hours of light but pay attention to the temperature. Tomatoes are going to want their environment to be really warm, so keep the temperature between 75F and 80F. At night time you will want to drop the temperature to 70F. Regarding the soil, tomatoes enjoy a pH level between 6.0 and 6.8. Where tomatoes especially demand attention is their humidity level. Your plants are going to want a humidity level between 80% and 90%. This massive level is not going to be possible without a humidifier and some careful attention. During the night, this level drops down around 65% to 75%. The reason they want such a high level is due to the fact that tomatoes are primarily made of water. Tomato plants use water to keep the leaves and stem healthy and to produce the tomatoes themselves. They need so much water that the roots aren't able to keep up with the demand, and so they need to rely on transpiration to pull it out of the atmosphere.

INDOOR GARDENING

Try to keep the humidity right in the middle, at 85%, or on the slightly lower end, around say 82%. This is because going above 90% can lead to the tomatoes suffocating. While they want plenty of water molecules in their environment, too many of these molecules will prevent the transpiration process from activating as it's supposed to. A humidity level that is too high leaves your plants at risk of flower drop, where blossoms fall off before maturing into fruit.

After the vegetative stage in the life cycle comes the flowering period. By keeping the light on for 18 to 24 hours a day, we are tricking the tomato plant into staying in the vegetative growth stage. Changing the lighting conditions of your tomatoes so that they begin by only getting 8 to 12 hours of light a day will trick them into thinking it's time to commence flowering. After you make this change in their lighting, you can expect to have fully grown tomatoes within the next 80 days. If you are planning to move your tomato plants to a larger container, then you will want to do this a few weeks before forcing them into flowering. This way, they have plenty of time to get used to their new home before they start to go through these changes. Once they have begun to flower, continue feeding them an NPK balanced fertilizer for the first two or three weeks. Then, following that stage, you are going to want to change to a fertilizer with less nitrogen and more potassium and phosphorus, as these nutrients are more valuable for the flowering and fruiting phases of a tomato's life.

You are going to need to keep a close eye on your plants during this phase, particularly giving your attention to the flowers. You are going to need to start daily pollination from the point when the flowers first open up. The tomato flower has two primary parts involved in the pollination process. The first is the anthers (male) in the middle, and the second is the carpels (female), which are green pieces around the bud. The anthers of a plant primarily store their pollen on the outside, as this biological feature allows the pollen to be carried by the wind to pollinate the flowers. Tomatoes are a little more complicated, as their pollen is stored inside the anthers rather than on the outside. It is going to require vibration to get the pollen out of the anthers. In nature, this is achieved through the frequency of vibration that a honey bee buzzes. We can imitate this by using an electric toothbrush along the branches. Unlike strawberries or peaches, we aren't directly pollinating the flowers ourselves. Instead, what we do with tomatoes is vibrate them so that the pollen comes out and self-pollinates. This lack of control is why it is best to do this practice every day until the flowers turn into tomatoes. The other reason to do it so frequently is to produce more delicious tomatoes. The more pollen that manages to fertilize the plant, the more seeds there will be in the tomatoes themselves, and this means a much richer and tastier product. Once the tomatoes begin to grow, simply continue to look after the plant just as you have been doing, and harvest them when they are a bright and even red.

Cultivating Cucumbers

As with any plant, the first step is to decide what kind you are interested in growing. All sorts of cucumbers grow vines that like to climb all over what is around them. These don't necessarily require a trellis, but most growers want to train them to one to keep them orderly. Cucumbers are also known for having long taproots that dig deep into the soil. Varieties which forego this feature make for better plants when it comes to indoor gardening since there is only so far down the plant can dig into a container. A cucumber of the bush variety will have a much more contained growth, and that makes it a good fit for indoor gardeners. Once you have your seeds chosen, simply go ahead and plant them directly. Cucumber seeds have softer shells that don't require any extra work to start germinating. You can expect to see the seedlings poking out of the soil in about ten days.

Much like tomatoes, cucumbers prefer to have a source of continuous light. This extra light allows the cucumber seedlings to grow faster and more abundantly. If you are unable to provide them with continuous light, then simply light them for as long as you possibly can, with a minimum of eight hours of lighting a day. Transplant them into a larger container after they have been sticking out of the soil for a week or so. In terms of earth, cucumbers can grow in most potting mixtures, but they prefer loose soil with good drainage and plenty of organic plant matter (compost) to provide them with nutrition. They like to have a pH level between 6.0 and 7.0. A temperature between 65F and 75F during the day is ideal; just remember to drop that down to between 60F and 70F at night. In terms of humidity, cucumbers are rather unique in their needs. During the day, they like to have their humidity in the range of 60% to 70%. At night, they want a higher humidity level, somewhere in the range of 70% to 90%. While you can blast cucumbers with 24 hours of light while they are in the early stages of their growth, you will want to dial this back to 8 hours of light as they move towards their fruiting stage.

Cucumbers are very thirsty plants, as you might have guessed by their love of high humidity levels. As your cucumbers begin to fruit, they will require even more water. Use the finger test every day to ensure that the soil is moist. If you find that the top inch is dry, it's time to water them again immediately. Letting your cucumbers go thirsty is a recipe for disaster, so don't neglect this aspect of their care. You should also feed your cucumbers with a liquid fertilizer once every couple of weeks. An NPK balanced fertilizer is good, but what is extremely helpful to their wellbeing, is to provide them with a higher nitrogen supply, while still being mindful that the pH level stays between 6.0 and 7.0.

In keeping with the rest of the plants we've looked at throughout the book, when cucumbers flower, they have both male and female parts. There will be many more male flowers than female flowers. You can tell the female flowers apart because they will have tiny cucumbers growing behind them. To pollinate the females, you should remove a male flower from the plant and carefully peel back its petals as they store pollen on the inside just like tomatoes. With the petals peeled back, you can use the male flower like a brush. Simply run the male flower across the female flower. For the best possible results (aka the tastiest!), use a male flower from one cucumber plant to pollinate the females of another plant and vice versa. .

Continue to provide your cucumbers with plenty of water and nutrients while they fruit, and you will have fresh cucumbers in no time. From sprouting to harvesting often takes about sixty days. To harvest, simply pluck off the fully grown cucumbers by cutting the stem with your shears. Make your cut about three-quarters of an inch to an inch and a quarter from the top of the cucumber. Any cucumbers that are taking on a yellow color should be cut off and thrown out, as these unhealthy cucumbers will continue to grow and divert precious energy from the good ones.

Growing Edible Eggplants

Eggplants are originally from India, yet they have become a staple of dinner tables all across North America. While they can be hard to grow in your backyard, growing them indoors is a much easier experience and one that adds a nice variety to your indoor garden. As with any indoor garden, since space is an issue, it is always best to choose a variety of eggplant that isn't going to take up too much room. The little fingers, or fairy tale types, are delicious plants that don't need too much space. Starting with your small seed trays, fill them up with your potting soil and dig two small holes about a quarter-inch deep. Drop a seed or two into each of these and cover with soil. Remember not to pack the soil too tightly. Water the seeds immediately and then cover with a lid or plastic wrap. Keep these seeds

INDOOR GARDENING

at 75F with 12 to 14 hours of light per day. Remove the plastic wrap and use your spray bottle to mist the top of the soil on a daily basis. Use the finger test to see if the top inch is dry, and water when it is. Reapply the plastic wrap cover afterward. In one or two weeks, you will see seedlings sprouting out of the soil, at which point you can remove the plastic wrap or lids.

Judge which seedling is the stronger of the two and transplant this one into a larger container when it has grown to a height of roughly an inch. Eggplants like soil that drains quickly, with plenty of holes in the pot to allow for water to come out. Since they are originally from India, they enjoy drier conditions than many of the more traditional garden vegetables. Make sure there is plenty of compost in your potting soil mix to provide them with lots of nutrients. You will also want to spike a small trellis into the pot to help support the weight of the eggplant as it grows. Now that they have been transplanted, they should be comfortable in a slightly warmer environment, somewhere between 75F and 85F. Continue using the finger test to check the soil and water when the top inch is dry. You should also continue misting the plants every day. Eggplants like the humidity to be right in the middle, so aim to give them about 50% humidity. Feed them with an NPK balanced liquid fertilizer, and make sure you do this every week.

Wait for your eggplants to blossom and then use a brush to pollinate the flowers. Eggplants pretty much reproduce the same way that strawberries do, so go over each of the flowers at least twice to ensure you have done it comprehensively. You will see the eggplant itself begin to grow. These plants have a longer life cycle compared to the others we've looked at, so you can expect it to take upwards of 100 days before they are ready to harvest. You will know the time is right when the skin of the eggplant is a deep purple color with a glossy shine, almost like a fresh coat of metallic paint.

Chapter Summary

- Indoor tomatoes should be a dwarf species, such as a cherry or plum tomato. Some varieties often grown indoors include pink ping pong, Siberia, micro tom, totem, red robin, or patio tomatoes.

- Tomatoes take between 50 to 90 days to grow from flowering to harvest. Chemical processes can speed this up, but the resulting tomatoes won't taste as good.

- You may want to add hydrated lime to your potting mix when it comes to tomatoes, as this will introduce more calcium. This element also helps prevent blossom end rot.

- Tomato seeds don't need to be prepared before you plant them. Simply plant the seeds, water them, cover the containers in plastic wrap, and wait for the seedlings to start poking through the soil. A temperature of 80F is perfect for germination. You can expect seedlings in one or two weeks.

- Transplant tomato seedlings when they are an inch and a half tall, choosing the healthiest of the seedlings to move. Throughout this period, the plants will want between 18 to 24 hours of light as they grow nice and large.

- Use a liquid fertilizer with lots of nitrogen during the vegetative stage. Keep the temperature between 75F and 80F, dropping the warmth down to 70F at night. Maintain a pH level between 6.0 and 6.8 with a humidity level between 80% and 90% during the day, and 65% to 75% at night. It is best to try to keep the humidity in the middle; too high or too low will damage the plants.

- Tomato plants need to be forced to flower when grown indoors. You can accomplish this by changing their lighting from between 18 to 24 hours to between 8 and 12 hours a day. You can expect to be eating your tomatoes 80 days from when you forced them to flower. Flowering tomatoes will want an NPK balanced fertilizer for the first couple weeks before switching to a fertilizer with less nitrogen and more potassium and phosphorus.

- As soon as the flowers begin to open up on your tomato plants, you are going to start pollinating them. In order to properly pollinate tomatoes, you will need to vibrate the flowers by using a tool such as an electric toothbrush. So long as you vibrate each flower, they will take care of the rest of the pollination process. Just make sure to do this every day until the tomatoes begin to grow; this will result in a tastier, meatier harvest.

- Cucumbers are known for having long taproots and growing lots of vines, so they will require a trellis and a deep container. Cucumbers of the bush variety will take up less space, making them ideal for indoor gardeners.

INDOOR GARDENING

- Cucumbers like to have light at all times. If you can't provide 24/7 light, then make sure you give them a minimum of 8 hours a day. Cucumbers also tend to want a pH level of between 6.0 and 7.0 and a temperature between 65F and 75F for the day and 60F and 70F at night. Their humidity level goes up at night, too, as they want between 60% and 70% during the day and a whopping 70% to 90% at night.

- Cucumbers require lots of water, so make sure to give them something to drink whenever the top inch of the soil is dry. Mix in a weekly treatment with a liquid fertilizer that is NPK balanced. Cucumbers also need lots of nitrogen, so you may consider feeding them a little extra as part of your fertilizer routine.

- Cucumbers need some help pollinating. Remove a male flower from the plant and peel back the petals to expose the pollen. This flower can now be used as a brush to put the pollen onto the female flowers directly. Cucumber plants benefit most by using the male of one plant to fertilize the females for another.

- You can expect to be eating your cucumbers within roughly sixty days or so after they first start to sprout.

- Eggplants don't need any extra work to plant, just drop a few seeds into a hole, and provide them with a temperature of 75F and 12 to 24 hours of light a day. You will want to mist them daily throughout this period as well.

- Eggplants require soil that drains quickly, but they can stand drier conditions than many of the other garden vegetables you will grow indoors. Provide a temperature between 75F and 85F as they grow, watering them only when the top inch is dry. However, you will still want to continue misting the plants on a daily basis. Use an NPK balanced fertilizer on a weekly basis.

- Use a brush to pollinate the flowers of the eggplant in the same manner that you would with strawberries. It will take upwards of 100 days before your eggplants are ready to be harvested, making them one of the slowest crops that you'll grow indoors.

In the next chapter, you will learn how to grow herbs like thyme, mint, or rosemary indoors. While herbs are often at the back of the queue in the minds of indoor gardeners, they can add some terrific flavors to your meals and take your cooking to the next level. They also grow very well indoors, with many growers beginning their exploration of gardening with herbs before moving onto vegetables or fruits.

CHAPTER SIX

PLANTING HEALTHY HERBS

While fruits and vegetables may be what most readily comes to mind when considering an indoor garden, you shouldn't overlook the value of cultivating your own herbs. Many gardeners first get into indoor gardening by starting a small herb garden. They're easy to care for and don't take up a lot of space. Of course, you can always scale up the size of a herb garden so that it takes up a lot of room, but, when compared to peach trees or eggplants, these little plants are downright tiny.

But they provide more than their fair share of flavor and aroma. While a herb garden won't put a full meal on your dinner table, it will make the food on that plate taste fantastic. In this chapter, we will look at growing a couple of the most common and versatile herbs. But before we do, let us first turn our attention towards why these herbs make for such a compelling addition to any indoor garden.

The Benefits of Herbs

Herbs are mostly thought of as a kind of spice, a plant that alters a dish to give the taste some extra depth. When you consider how many recipes call for mint, dill, basil, sage, rosemary, cilantro, or thyme, it is easy to see why herbs are so strongly associated with flavor. This reason alone is enough for many people to want to start their personal herb gardens; they are low maintenance, fun to grow, and mighty tasty. If this were the only property that these small plants possessed, it would still be well worth the trouble of cultivating them. But there is a whole world of health benefits that comes from adding herbs to your diet (and your garden). Looking at just a handful of these benefits will make it crystal clear how powerful these plants are. Remember that this is far from a comprehensive list, and there are even more benefits and more varieties of herbs than could conceivably fit in this book. They really are that impressive!

Sage is an earthy tasting herb that comes in two common forms, Salvia officinalis (plain) and Salvia lavandulaefolia (Spanish sage). A member of the mint family, small amounts of sage are used in quite a few dishes to give added zest to the natural flavor of the food. As little as one teaspoon of sage packs a great many vitamins and minerals, including 10% of the daily recommended vitamin K. It's also loaded with more than 160 different polyphenols which the body uses as antioxidants; some of these are believed to improve brain health, and are thought to lower an individual's risk of contracting cancer. Even if sage didn't do anything else, it would be an amazing little herb. But it's also been linked to reducing dental plaque and cavities, alleviating the symptoms of menopause, lowering blood sugar levels, and reducing LDL cholesterol. There are also studies showing that sage can be used in the treatment of diarrhea, improving the overall health of bones, and even reducing wrinkles and other signs of skin aging.

As mentioned earlier, sage is a member of the mint family. Perhaps the most well-known member of that family is peppermint, which is a staple ingredient of countless candies, teas, and extracts. The most common use of peppermint is to freshen your breath (that's why mints are offered after meals, and why it's also commonly used to flavor toothpaste), but this only scratches the surface of the benefits this aromatic herb offers. Another reason that peppermint is offered after a meal is due to the effect it has on the digestive system. It can relieve such unpleasant symptoms as indigestion, gas, and bloating, as it relaxes the muscles in the gastrointestinal tract, and has even been shown to reduce symptoms associated with IBS. Because of the effects it has on muscles, it's been used to treat tension headaches, and it has been linked to a reduction in headache pain when applied locally as an oil. Peppermint also has antiviral and antibacterial properties that help to open up your sinuses when they have been clogged due to colds. Peppermint has been linked to reduction in fatigue and to an improvement in energy levels. It seems to be effective in easing menstrual cramps, improving mental concentration, and helping with allergies related to seasonal conditions. Plus, there are studies showing that peppermint can reduce hunger pangs and therefore assist in weight loss. It's been used to promote restful sleep. It even appears to be good at killing off the harmful bacteria responsible for harmful infections such as E. coli or salmonella. So you can see, this aromatic herb has far more attributes than a pleasant taste.

Thyme is another of the mint family, which is arguably one of the most beneficial and wide-ranging families of plants on this planet outside of the papaveraceae group.

Often used to spice meals, there are actually more than 400 varieties of thyme. Their use dates back to the ancient Egyptians who used the plant as part of their embalming practices, and the ancient Greeks who burned it as a form of incense because of its attractive aroma. In regards to health benefits, thyme has been shown in animal studies to reduce the heart rate of rodents with high blood pressure, as well as to reduce the level of cholesterol in the same subjects. The use of thyme oil was shown to boost benign feelings in human subjects because of the active ingredient carvacrol. Carvacrol has a direct effect on the way that neurons in the brain function and regular use has been linked to an improvement in feelings of happiness and wellbeing. When the leaves of thyme are crushed to produce oil, the resulting juice can be taken orally to alleviate sore throats and to suppress coughing. The effect can also be achieved by adding thyme leaves to your tea; you can just pluck the leaves straight off your indoor plant. Not only does it help to reduce sore throats and coughs, regular use in tea or meals can help to strengthen your immune system in preventing colds in the first place. Thyme is a good source for vitamin C, copper, fiber, manganese, vitamin A, and iron, making this simple herb a super-healthy addition to your dinner. Beyond health benefits, thyme is often used as an ingredient in pesticides, and studies have shown that it even repels mosquitoes. Keeping thyme near your other plants can help to deter pests, though it is most productive in this manner when the leaves have been rubbed together or crushed to release their oil. Also, that same oil can be employed to help battle mold, since it has fungicidal properties that make it a useful ingredient in natural disinfectants and cleaners.

As you are probably starting to see a theme emerging here, let's only look at the benefits of one more herb. Far from just being a pretty name, rosemary is an aromatic herb that has been used extensively in traditional Hindu medicine. It is native to the Mediterranean and South America, but found its way into the North American market, and has become a staple of herb gardens all across the continent. It is part of the lamiaceae family that includes mint, basil, and oregano. Used to spice food or brew tea, this powerful little herb has a great many antioxidants that have been linked to protecting the body from inflammation damage and a decrease in the risk of cancer, heart disease, and type 2 diabetes. Rosemary also has anti-inflammatory properties because of its polyphenolic compounds. Other elements in rosemary have antimicrobial properties that enable the body to fight off deadly infections. This is one reason why traditional medicine has made use of it for centuries. Blood sugar levels have improved in individuals who use it, and research suggests it is beneficial in improving mood and memory. If you want to improve your memory and concentration, you can take it orally, but studies show that simply inhaling the aroma improves these areas as well. The link between rosemary and brain health doesn't stop there. Rosemary brewed into tea seems to have a positive effect in preventing brain cells from dying. Ongoing research suggests it may be beneficial in recovering from such traumatic brain injuries as strokes or reducing the effects of neurodegenerative diseases such as Alzheimer's. Rosemary has been linked to improving eye health and slowing age-related eye diseases, and both delaying and reducing the severity of cataracts. Along with all these terrific qualities, it's also beneficial in helping reduce the after-effects of a heart attack, reducing indigestion, and improving weight loss. Possibly, it may even improve hair growth; research has certainly shown it reduces hair *loss*, but there are more studies required to see if it promotes growth, though many people have claimed it does.

Looking at less than five herbs, we have seen that they have health benefits for nearly every area of the human body. Bear in mind: it should not be thought that the use of herbs removes the need for medical care - this would be a mistaken idea. Rather, the health benefits of these herbs should be thought of as supplemental to proper health care. We only looked at four herbs here, but there are more than 200,000 different subspecies within the designation of herb. This massive variety leaves a great deal of room for more benefits to be discovered through research. It also means there are more flavor combinations for your meals than could be listed in this book or even a hundred such books. In order to experience those, you're just going to have to start growing your own and experimenting with your dishes. So let's now turn our attention over to raising herbs as a part of our indoor garden.

Growing Thyme Indoors

In addition to the health benefits we explored above, thyme makes a wonderful addition to your salads, as a garnish on meat, or as an ingredient in your pasta sauces. As you will come to see with most herbs, thyme is very easy to grow, and many people have been successful in raising thyme plants just by letting them stand on a windowsill. The biggest trick to learn when it comes to growing herbs (and thyme is no different here), is figuring out how to pick it for use while keeping it alive so it can continue to produce.

The most common way that thyme is grown is through propagation. We can do this by taking cuttings from the tips of leaves and planting these, or it can be done by dividing a mature plant. To divide a mature plant, simply remove your thyme plant from its container, and carefully pull the root ball and the stems apart so that you now have two root balls rather than one. Replant the original ball in the same container and plant the new ball in a second container. With that simple move, you now have two thyme plants. If you want to grow from seed, then all you need to do is scatter thyme seeds in your chosen container, cover them with soil, water them, and then cover the container with plastic wrap. The bowl should be set in a warm location to wait for germination to take place. Despite being a soft-shelled seed, thyme plants can take anywhere from seven to eighty-four days to begin germinating. What this does mean is you really won't know if the seeds were viable or not until almost a hundred days after planting. This uncertainty dissuades many people from growing thyme from seed, especially when propagating is so simple and quick.

Thyme is often grown on windowsills because it prefers to have lots of bright light. It benefits from having direct sunlight, though, if it isn't feasible in your area, it can be compensated for by your grow lights. Growing thyme using electric lights can be a smart choice as they will let you raise this herb all-year round rather than seasonally. Thyme likes plenty of water but not all at once. You need to allow the soil to dry out before watering it again, as too much moisture will cause thyme to rot. Your best bet is to use the finger test to a depth of two inches, watering only when both inches are dry. Thyme has a resistance to the harmful effects of drought, so it is better for it to be too dry than for it to be too moist. Because of how harmful moisture is, thyme should be planted in a lightweight soil with plenty of pockets for air to move through and quick drainage. Likewise, thyme does not require any extra humidity as this also promotes rot; you should grow thyme away from your indoor fruits and vegetables in an area that has plenty of airflow. Fertilize thyme on a weekly or bi-weekly basis with an NPK balanced liquid fertilizer applied to the soil rather than the plant.

Raising Rosemary

As rosemary comes from the Mediterranean, its environmental preferences reflect that climate. It's a herb that can tolerate droughts and craves plenty of direct sunlight. Much like thyme, rosemary is more often than not purchased as an already growing plant, rather than in seed form. Choosing to grow from seed is as simple a procedure as thyme; merely plant them and wait for them to grow. Be aware they also take a long time to grow from seed to dinner-ready. It is far easier to purchase rosemary as a plant, and then take leaf tip cuttings to propagate a new plant.

You will notice that we didn't bother talking about repotting thyme. That's because it's a small plant, and the only time it ever needs to be repotted is if you purchased it from a store and decided you wanted to move it to a different container. Rosemary, on the other hand, can grow up to four feet in height and takes up much more space than thyme. If you want to keep rosemary at a smaller size, then you need to repot it during the spring and prune the size of the root down by a third before planting it back into a container of the same size. If you do want it to keep growing larger, simply wait until spring and transplant it into a bigger container.

Rosemary likes lots of sunlight, between 8 to 14 hours a day. The rule of thumb with most of the Mediterranean herbs is that the more light you can provide them, the healthier they will be. Just as with thyme, rosemary will begin to rot if it has to deal with too much moisture. Use the finger test to make sure that the soil is dry before watering. This is a case where overwatering will kill the plant, but underwatering will hardly affect it at all. Since it loves bright light and direct sunlight, this means it wants plenty of heat. Keep the temperature between 50F and upwards of 80F, sometimes even higher. Just remember that the hotter the temperature is, the more airflow will be required to keep it healthy. Plant rosemary in a soil that drains quickly, and use a liquid fertilizer weekly, applying to the earth rather than directly on to the plant itself.

While rosemary has plenty of issues that may affect it, such as too much moisture causing it to rot, the biggest problem that growers face is preventing powdery mildew from taking hold. This unpleasant fungal disease is prone to strike plants that are overly moist, under-lit, or lacking in proper air circulation. You can tell powdery mildew from its white, powder-like appearance. It looks almost as if someone has sprinkled flour over the leaves of your plant. Treating this mildew can be a real pain. Since rosemary is a herb, it is primarily grown with the intention of being ingested by humans. Therefore, if it should acquire a disease, you don't want to treat the problem with harmful chemicals that will make you sick. If you spot any powdery mildew on your plant, you should immediately remove all of the parts that have been infected and dispose of them outdoors. Next, reduce how much you are watering the plant and ensure that it is getting enough sun and circulation. Neem oil should be used on your plant regularly, long before any signs of the mildew. After all, prevention is always better than cure. If you have been applying neem oil and your rosemary has still been infected, then increase the regularity of use and supplement with baking soda as a natural remedy.

Maintaining Mint

INDOOR GARDENING

Mint is a particularly forgiving plant, able to grow just about anywhere you may want to put it. Of course, it does have its preferences, but as far as plants go, it is remarkably flexible in a way that makes it a good choice for first-time gardeners setting up an indoor operation. But the versatility that it shows in growing is vastly outperformed by the versatility it demonstrates when it comes to consumption. Mint leaves can be used to flavor teas or relishes, or add a delicious layer of flavor to yogurt or ice cream. It is used to garnish meat dishes, or it can be tossed in a salad, and there are many drinks, both alcoholic and non-alcoholic, that use it as a core ingredient. When you combine this adaptability with the health benefits mint has, it is easy to see why everyone would benefit from adding a bit of mint to their garden.

As far as containers go, mint will need to be housed in one that has drainage holes at the bottom to help it dry out properly. Unlike rosemary or thyme, mint enjoys more moisture, but too much is still going to impact its health negatively. If you need to make a choice between a wide container or a deep one, go with the wide one, as mint grows and spreads in a lateral fashion rather than a vertical one. In fact, mint spreads so quickly that if you were to plant it in an outdoor garden, then you would have to be extra vigilant in ensuring it doesn't choke out the other plants in the bed. We avoid this tricky problem by growing it indoors.

Mint likes to have a pH level between 6.0 and 7.0, and it grows best when the potting mixture has plenty of sand mixed in to promote quick drainage. However, like many herbs, the pH level is far less important to mint than it is to fruits or vegetables. Herbs have a tendency to be resilient to problems involving the richness of their soil. That said, if the pH level is going to be off, then it is better to be too low rather than too high as an overly high pH level can promote extremely troublesome fungal infections. For the best results, replace the soil once a year. Mint will suck out all of the nutrients quickly, and adding compost will only maintain the soil's longevity up to a point. It is also strongly recommended that you add a top layer of mulch to create a defense against harmful bacteria and that you reduce the frequency of watering.

The most common way of growing a new mint plant is to take a clipping of the stem from slightly above a leaf.

Take this clipping and place it into a glass of clean water, or into a perlite and vermiculite mixture that has been moistened ahead of time. Ensure that each cutting is a few inches in length and that it has some new growth. After a week or two, you will notice roots beginning to form at the bottom of the clipping, at which point you can then repot it. Other ways to grow mint are to divide them by removing the plant from its container, splitting the root ball into two, and then planting each ball into a separate bowl. To grow mint from seeds, you will need to scatter seeds throughout a container, frequently mist the soil, and wait for upwards of three months for germination to take place. Mint seedlings are especially fragile, so great care must be taken when handling them or even when watering them. As a rule of thumb, growing from seed has the lowest success rate while dividing has the highest. Dividing is the quickest way to get new plants up, followed close behind by cuttings. In the time it takes to grow a seed, you could have started new plants from cuttings three times over.

Mint enjoys the sun, but it likes to have partial shading rather than direct light. That said, it likes to have light throughout the entire day. If you need to provide an electric lighting setup for your mint plants, then you are going to want to get the lights very close to the plant itself. Expect to give mint between 8 to 10 hours of light in a day. When it comes to watering, mint wants to be kept moist, so the best way to check if it is time to water is to do a reduced version of the finger test and simply check the top of the soil. If it is dry to the touch, then it is time to water. Mint also enjoys a higher humidity than the other herbs we looked at, with around 70% being ideal. If you cannot provide your mint with humidity at this level, then regular misting will help to provide it with enough moisture in the atmosphere. Mint doesn't particularly need much fertilizing, although a bi-weekly treatment with an NPK balanced solution applied to the soil can help. Be mindful of how much you are fertilizing mint and the smell and taste of it. Too much fertilizer will reduce the flavor.

While mint is quite easy to look after, it does have one extra step that others don't. Mint will bend towards the source of light, giving it an unhealthy appearance, almost as if it were wilting. While this isn't in any way unhealthy, it is unseemly. Rotate the container twice a week to prevent this lopsided look.

Chapter Summary

- While herbs are primarily added to dishes and consumed for their flavors, they have a vast range of health benefits that make them a wonderful addition to any home garden.

- Sage is jam-packed full of vitamins and minerals, with more than 160 polyphenols. It has been linked to reductions in cases of cancer, and improvement in brain health, as well as dental health, reduction of menopause symptoms, lower blood sugar, and lower levels of LDL cholesterol. Sage is also used in treating diarrhea and improving bone and skin health.

- Peppermint freshens your breath and promotes digestive health. It is also used in treating headaches and has both antiviral and antibacterial properties. Peppermint has been linked to improved brain health and concentration, reduced menstrual cramps, improvements in sleep, and it helps to kill off harmful bacteria.

- Thyme reduces blood pressure and harmful cholesterol, boosts mood and mental wellbeing, alleviates sore throats and coughing, is filled with lots of nutrients, and can even be used to repel pests that want to turn your garden into a snack bar.

- Rosemary helps repair inflammation damage, reduces the risk of cancer, type 2 diabetes, and heart disease. It has been shown to help with blood pressure, mood and memory function, and even help prevent brain cells from dying. Rosemary has been linked to other areas of health: these include the eyes, the hair, and recovering from heart attacks.

- There are more than 200,000 different subspecies of herbs, meaning you have an endless variety to experiment with for reasons of health and flavor.

- Thyme is easiest to grow through propagation, cutting off clippings to create new plants, or splitting the root ball to produce two identical plants. Growing from seeds takes months and has a much lower success rate.

- Thyme likes to have lots of light and plenty of water, but the soil should be left to dry completely between waterings as too much will cause rot. Keep thyme in an area with low humidity and earth that will promote fast drainage.

- Rosemary likes hot areas, lots of sun, and dry periods between watering. Like thyme, it is best to create new plants through propagation instead of growing from seed. Rosemary grows several feet in length, so clipping the roots once a year should be done to keep it at a consistent size.

- Rosemary shouldn't be exposed to too much moisture, as this promotes both rot and the growth of powdery mildew. Provide plenty of airflow to help reduce this, and remove any infected leaves as soon as you notice them. Treatment with neem oil and baking soda together can help to defeat an infection if caught early.

- Mint likes lots of drainage in its soil and lots of moisture. Check the top of the soil to see if it is dry, watering when it is. A daily misting will help to ensure that mint gets the 70% humidity it desires. Plenty of nutrients in the soil is fine for mint, as it likes a pH level between 6.0 and 7.0. It is better to go below 6.0 than it is to go over 7.0, as mint can withstand lower pH levels far better than it can higher.

- Keep mint in partial shade for 8 to 10 hours, providing it with an NPK balanced fertilizer once every few weeks. Too much fertilizer will drain away the flavor, making the taste test a good way to see if you need to reduce your fertilizing schedule. Rotate mint twice a week to prevent it from growing lopsided.

In the next chapter, you will learn the most common mistakes that new growers make. We will consider faults such as failing to keep the growing space clean or ignoring warning signs of nutrient burn, infection, or poor environmental conditions. By becoming aware of such pitfalls, you can be sure you'll avoid these costly mistakes and keep your garden healthy and beautiful.

CHAPTER SEVEN

COMMON MISTAKES AND HOW TO AVOID THEM

When it comes to gardening, there are a great many errors that growers are prone to make when they start out. In fact, truth to tell, there are many gardeners who continue to make mistakes despite having acquired years of experience. The most common reason that mistakes are made is ignorance. Some people simply think that if they can raise carrots, then they can raise lettuce, or if they can grow an orange tree, then they understand how to take care of mint. This attitude ignores the subtle (and not so subtle) differences between plants, and simply reduces a vast topic into too rigid a formula. When this happens, dead plants and poor harvests are prone to follow.

While the chances are that you will make mistakes of your own during the early stages of creating your indoor fruit, vegetable, or herb garden, this chapter aims to make you aware of the most common mistakes that new growers are likely to make. By being aware of these mistakes, you reduce your level of ignorance, and you increase your chances of avoiding them yourself. Now, this doesn't mean that you will, by default, avoid these mistakes simply because you read this chapter. But it does mean that you have the knowledge necessary to avoid them so long as you act on it. In the world of growing, much as with life in general, we are required to act on our knowledge if we want to see the best results.

Not Doing Your Research

We've looked at a handful of plants throughout this book, and, while some of them share similarities (such as thyme and rosemary), they all have notable differences in how much light, water, fertilizer, space, and humidity they want, as well as which nutrients they like best, and what pH level they require to stay healthy. If there can be this much of a difference between the small handful that we were able to look at, then you can only imagine how much variety there is across the plant kingdom. Not only that, but keep in mind that different subspecies of plants often have their own preferences that, while similar to each other, can show a great deal of variation. All this adds up to the fact that you should never make an assumption about the needs of a plant.

Instead, do your research on your plants. If you have access to the internet, then a quick Google search will reveal link after link about how to raise whatever kind of fruit, vegetable, or herb you are considering. If you aren't very technologically savvy, then you should consider stopping in at your local gardening center and asking them for advice. The chances are good that you were going to get your seeds from them anyway, so why not pick their brains first to find out everything you need to know. Questions you should consider asking are: How often should I water this plant? What type of fertilizer do they need and how often do they need it? Does it take long to germinate? How long does it take to grow? When can I expect it to start fruiting? How much light does it want? Does it prefer direct sunlight or partial shade? What temperature should it be kept at? How much humidity does it require? What pH level will it need? Is there anything I should know about pollinating it by hand? Are there any health risks I should be aware of?

Asking questions and doing your research should be the very first step you take when considering growing something that is new to you. Before you even look up the price of seeds or seedlings, ask all the questions you need answering, whether or not you are capable of providing an ideal environment for this type of plant. Being prepared with information will save you money as you can avoid those that aren't a good fit, and you will also spare yourself the disappointment of watching a new plant wilt and die.

Growing Too Much At Once

When they're beginning, many people have big, grand plans for their indoor gardens. They're going to have lettuce and tomatoes, carrots and eggplants, a peach tree, some rosemary, and a bunch of mint. In theory, this sounds amazing. Who wouldn't want to have that much delicious food at their fingertips? But in practice, this is often a recipe for disaster.

The first issue that many people are going to run into by expanding too fast is the fact that things aren't growing as they thought. Just because you plant a seed, doesn't mean it is going to grow. It can be particularly discouraging for new gardeners when it happens once, but consider when it happens to several plants all at the same time. Furthermore, even if they do germinate, each plant is going to grow at a different rate, and this means that you will need to balance the needs of a number of different plants that are all at various stages of development. Pay special attention to the use of that word "balance." Gardening takes up your time and attention; you need to watch your plants to get a sense of how they are doing, and then adjust their care accordingly. While you might think that this will be quick and easy, many new gardeners are completely shocked at just how long this can take.

When you are starting, begin small and then expand as you become more comfortable with looking after a garden. While I would suggest starting with a single plant, many will find this to be too small to make it worth their time. If you need more, allow yourself two or three plants but limit yourself to this. Pick plants that have similar care routines and environmental requirements so that you can worry about building one environment, rather than fine-tuning several. Take these plants through to harvest before you add any more. That way, you know what is required for each step in the care process. Start slow, and add more as your skill and understanding increases. Approach it with a sensible attitude. Looked at this way, becoming proficient at gardening is not that different from any other skill.

Planting Seeds Too Close Together

When you are first putting seeds (or even seedlings) into a container, it will seem like there is an abundance of space. After all, seeds are super-tiny, and so you can put a whole whack of them in a container without it feeling like they are crowding each other out. While this is true at these early stages of growth, you will quickly come to regret this decision when your plants start to grow, and you realize that they have no space at all. But why is this a bad thing, necessarily?

First off, while you will notice the lack of space on top of the soil, it is really what is happening under the soil that is damaging your plants the most. Their roots are going to start to get tangled and fight to find their own space while they grow, and this is going to cause a number of issues that negatively affect their overall health. Those same roots are going to have to compete with each other for nutrients, and this means that all of your plants are going to be far less healthy when compared to those that get all the nutrients they need without a struggle. The struggle to fight for nutrients wastes energy, energy which would be better utilized in promoting growth. Stunted plants are one such result from being planted too close together.

Another factor to bear in mind is that pests and disease can much more easily spread from plant to plant when they are too close together. Moreover, they have more places to hide; it is much harder to see all the nooks and crannies of your plants when they obscure each other. Therefore it's evident that planting too close together creates more difficulties with pests and diseases and smaller harvests of less tasty food.

Not Checking for Pests or Cleaning for Disease

Speaking of pests - have you been checking for them? If not, then how do you know that your plants are still healthy? Just because you don't see pests when you look at your plants doesn't mean that they might not already be feeding off your plants. There are many telltale signs of infection such as discoloration in leaves, bumps or holes in the leaves, or leaves that have begun to wilt for no discernible reason. The longer an infestation takes hold, the more damage your plants will sustain, and they can only take so much before they give up and die.

You want to ensure your plants are free of infestation or infection; the simplest precaution is to check them daily. This takes up time, that resource many new growers discount when they decide to grow too many plants. While many pests can be detected on sight, there are more than a few that either hide or are invisible to the naked eye. If you see pests, you need to start treating your plants immediately. But you should also do spot tests on a daily basis to see if any such parasites are hiding. Use your rake to check the soil at the roots, as many pests lay eggs in the soil; the offspring of these eggs will, given the chance, chew away at the stem. Next, take a piece of paper towel or toilet paper, and wipe the bottoms of the leaves. If the paper comes away with streaks of blood, then there are pests you are going to have to deal with. There are many methods of dealing with pests, but you should do your research before embarking on any of them. Since fruits, vegetables, and herbs are all plants that we grow with the intention of eating, it's crucial to ensure that whatever pesticide or solution you use to treat your plants is not going to harm the food you eat.

While you are making it a habit to check for pests, you should also keep your eyes open for signs of disease. White powdery mildew, molds, discoloration, wilting branches, rotting fruit - all of these are signs that your plants have caught a disease. The first step in tackling most sicknesses is to cut away any infected parts and immediately dispose of them outdoors. Apply treatments to your plants after ensuring those treatments aren't harmful to humans.

There are several key steps you should take to avoid disease in the first place,. Apply neem oil on a weekly basis, even if there are no signs of infestation or infection. This is a preventative measure so that you won't have to deal with these annoyances. Also, keep a close eye on how much water and light the plants are getting to ensure that they aren't getting too little or too much. Next, check the pH level of the soil to make sure that they have enough nutrients, as too few can leave them sickly, and too many can cause nutrient burn. Finally, though just as importantly, make sure that dead plant matter is removed from the area. The compost that is used in the soil is fine, but leaves or branches that have fallen off the plants and are rotting in the general area are quite harmful. This rotting plant matter, when it isn't being used as part of a properly planned feeding system, can introduce harmful bacteria to your growing area. Always make sure you remove any dead or fallen plant matter from the growing area and wash your hands first before you start handling your plants.

Chapter Summary

- The most significant cause of mistakes that new indoor gardeners encounter usually originates from either ignorance or simplistic assumption.

- Every plant is different, and this means that every plant has different needs, though some elements of those needs may be similar to others. Even within a particular kind of plant, the various subspecies may have vastly different environmental needs compared to each other.

- There are a great many questions that you should ask when you are first considering planting a type of plant that you haven't worked with before. These can often be answered by asking these questions of Google or through approaching a knowledgeable employee at your local gardening center.

- Researching should be the first step you take before starting with any new plants.

- Beginners often aim big and plant all sorts of different plants with the intention of enjoying them on their dinner plate in the near future. What they overlook is the difficulty associated with maintaining multiple types of plants simultaneously, and how much time and energy it takes to look after a full garden.

- It is always smarter to start with one to three plants and bring them from seed to harvest, before branching out and increasing the size of your growing operation. A modest beginning will give you a sense of how much effort it takes to properly grow your fruits, vegetables, or herbs.

- When you have your plants too close together, their roots begin to fight each other for nutrients. This wastes energy that would be better employed in growing into healthy adult plants. Planting too close together will leave you with small, sickly plants.

- Planting too close together also makes it easier for pests and diseases to spread from one plant to the next. They won't need to travel as far, and there are more parts of the plants that are obscured from the scrutiny of the gardener.

- Signs like discoloration, bumps, or holes in your leaves are telltale signs of either infestation or infection. Many pests can be tricky to spot if you aren't specifically looking for them and, if left untreated, they can kill your plants.

- Check the soil and the bottom of your leaves to see if there are any pests hiding where you can't see them. Make it a habit to check daily.

- Infection can spread quickly through a plant, and any infected leaves or branches should be cut off and disposed of outdoors. Dead plant matter around the growing space can introduce harmful bacteria into the environment. You should always clean up and tidy your growing area every day, washing your hands afterward before you touch your plants again.

FINAL WORDS

Creating an indoor garden is no more difficult than growing one outdoors. Indeed, the level of control that we have over an indoor environment makes it easier in many ways. Rain, drought, chill, or snow no longer mean death for your plants, and through the use of electric lights, you are able to provide enough "sunlight" to ensure your plants stay healthy and happy.

In order to properly grow plants indoors, you are going to need to invest more money into ensuring you have a proper environment for them. Nonetheless, a lot of this money is used in the earliest parts of the setup, such as purchasing grow lights, fans, or humidifiers. Once you have made the investment in this gear, you will be able to reuse it again and again for crop after crop. Viewed that way, the investment becomes easier to justify. Not only that but if you decide that indoor gardening isn't for you, then you can resell this equipment to make back some of your money. Just remember to start small when you begin; otherwise, the cost of your investment, and the time you need to commit will be much higher.

As we deal with issues like global warming and changing environments, indoor gardening will continue to grow in popularity. In the future, it seems likely that a substantial proportion of our foods will be grown and raised inside, rather than outside. What this means is that the skills and

INDOOR GARDENING

knowledge you have gained from this book are going to become more relevant to daily life, and more in demand in the coming years. Starting your indoor garden today will give you the practical experience you need to teach others how to start theirs. Not only is indoor gardening a great choice to be able to enjoy organically-grown fruits and vegetables from the comfort of your home, but it's also an investment in you and your family's future.

We have only been able to cover a small selection of the plants that you can grow indoors. You shouldn't feel limited to sticking to those that we have discussed throughout the book. Instead, you should take the lessons we've gone over here, and apply them to the fruits, vegetables, and herbs that most interest you. Just remember to do your research to ensure that you can provide the right environment for your plants, be they blueberries, basil, pumpkins, or anything else. Each plant is unique and you should respect it as such. With this attitude and a little attention, you will be able to grow anything your heart desires.

So what are you waiting for? Put this book down and go get your hands dirty tending to your own indoor fruit, vegetable, and herb garde

GREENHOUSE

A Comprehensive Guide to Cultivating Fruits, Vegetables, and Herbs for Beginners

Tom Gordon

GREENHOUSE

© Copyright 2019 - All rights reserved.

The content contained within this book may not be reproduced, duplicated or transmitted without direct written permission from the author or the publisher.

Under no circumstances will any blame or legal responsibility be held against the publisher, or author, for any damages, reparation, or monetary loss due to the information contained within this book. Either directly or indirectly.

Legal Notice:

This book is copyright protected. This book is only for personal use. You cannot amend, distribute, sell, use, quote or paraphrase any part, or the content within this book, without the consent of the author or publisher.

Disclaimer Notice:

Please note the information contained within this document is for educational and entertainment purposes only. All effort has been executed to present accurate, up to date, and reliable, complete information. No warranties of any kind are declared or implied. Readers acknowledge that the author is not engaging in the rendering of legal, financial, medical or professional advice. The content within this book has been derived from various sources. Please consult a licensed professional before attempting any techniques outlined in this book.

By reading this document, the reader agrees that under no circumstances is the author responsible for any losses, direct or indirect, which are incurred as a result of the use of information contained within this document, including, but not limited to, — errors, omissions, or inaccuracies.

INTRODUCTION

This comprehensive guide will provide you with a step-by-step procedure for setting up a greenhouse in your own backyard. The tutorial highlights the equipment and tools needed to build and successfully run your greenhouse garden.

As a beginner to greenhouse gardening, you're bound to make many mistakes, and this guide will help you avoid some of the errors made by other greenhouse farmers. You don't have to make the same mistakes while cultivating fruits, vegetables, and herbs in your garden.

You will learn how to manage the greenhouse, how to determine the right soil to cultivate vegetables, and how to improve the soil texture to produce maximum yields. You will also learn how to add fertilizers based on the soil pH value and increase soil concentration.

As a farmer, you may face several challenges like pest infection and diseases. In this guide, you we will go over how to manage and control pests in the greenhouse. This book will teach you how to know your crops are infected, about the various signs of different diseases, about the causes of these diseases, and how to prevent the spread of those diseases in your garden.

CHAPTER ONE

GREENHOUSE GARDENING

A **greenhouse** is a high-tech production facility or structure with a transparent roof material, like glass. The structure is suitable for growing seasonal plants or vegetables under regulated, climatic conditions.

If you're looking forward to growing fresh vegetables, fruits, and exotic herbs that can't survive under normal, seasonal conditions, then a greenhouse is the way to go. You can set up a greenhouse structure in your backyard to provide you with warm and stable environment for growing seasonal plants.

A greenhouse technology will protect your plants from harsh climatic conditions like wind, high temperatures, cold, extreme radiation, insects, and many plant diseases. The structure you build will provide fully controlled environmental conditions, making them ideal for product growth.

There are various types of greenhouses made with

different designs and styles to consider when planning to set up a greenhouse. Depending on your needs and budget, you can choose one of the following greenhouse forms, under glass or a polycarbonate structure, to start gardening with.

Why Cultivate in a Greenhouse

Greenhouses offer a lot of advantages to the owner and provide you with an ideal environment to extend your growing season. Some advantages you will gain through installing a greenhouse in your backyard include:

Having a longer growing season: A greenhouse can extend the growing season and allow you to plant all-year round vegetables in a controlled environment. It also gives you the freedom to plant crops at the beginning or at the end of the season.

Control climate conditions: A greenhouse protects your crops from harsh weather conditions. The structure provide shield to your crops from extreme temperatures, strong winds, and even frost. You can install temperature and heating control tools inside the structure to regulate the climate, and you can also install lighting equipment and vents for constant air circulation.

Grow a variety of plants: Greenhouses give you the opportunity to grow a wide variety of crops. If there are certain plants that don't do well in your location, which you can plant in your greenhouse. You can adjust the greenhouse conditions to meet the growing requirements of the plant.

Pest control: Growing vegetables, herbs, and fruits in a shielded area is one of the most effective methods in controlling pests from infecting your plants. The closed structure prevents pests and other insects from attacking the plants, required that you come up with the right preventive measures.

Fresh produce: You will be able to harvest fresh vegetables, fruits, and herbs from your garden at anytime, whenever you need them.

GREENHOUSE

Where to Start

Before buying or building your greenhouse, you need to determine how much space you need to grow your products and whether you need a *domestic* or *commercial* greenhouse. A greenhouse is a long-term investment; therefore, you need to be careful when making your selection for growing space. The space should be large enough to accommodate more plants in future, for example, if you want to plant vegetables or fruits, you need plenty of headroom and light.

You also need to do a research on the climate conditions, temperature, and moisture that would be suitable for growing your fruits, vegetables, and herbs of choice. This step is essential for the survival of your plants.

You need to plan for your planting schedule. A good plan should ensure you have constant supply of fruits and vegetables for all four seasons.

Greenhouses come in different styles that you can fit with several technological tools aimed at optimizing favorable climatic conditions for plant growth. Commercial greenhouses have computer-controlled equipment for cooling, heating, and lighting the structure. Different types of budget-friendly structures are available in the market, and you can build some of these structures within a day.

GREENHOUSE

Site Selection for the Greenhouse

Before selecting the type of greenhouse, you need to look at the following requirements for your vegetables, herbs, and fruit garden. These factors can apply to other farmers dealing with other types of specialized crops. The requirements are also important when planning to expand your greenhouse in the future.

Quality water: The type of crops grown, type of irrigation system, and other factors like the climate of the area determine the amount of water you need in your greenhouse. You should also carry out a test to determine the water quality in the area like the pH level, hardness, electrical conductivity, alkalinity, and any other dissolved elements in the water. Ensure you have constant supply of water within the area; generally, the total daily consumption per square foot should be 0.3 gallons.

Adequate land: You need at least two acres of land for the greenhouse, parking area, buffers, and any other facility needed in the area. An extra vacant land in the area is essential for expansion of your garden once the business grows. The land should have an excellent soil type for providing drainage.

Topography of the area: Greenhouses are always built facing south; therefore, when choosing the site location, you should look for the one with a gentle slope facing the south. This is great for harness solar energy and providing adequate lighting inside the greenhouse. A site with at least 1% to 2% slope will help you cut down costs on the preparation of the site.

Site orientation: The selected site should have great access to solar all day. This ensures you capture enough light energy for the process of photosynthesis. The site should also have shelter belts (trees and shrubs) at least to the north side to protect your crops from harsh weather like strong wind. Shelter belts not only protect the crops but can also help in energy conservation.

Accessibility: The area selected should be easily accessible by road. Setting up the greenhouse on a highway will ensure there is fast delivery of your produce. If it's on a busy road, there is a high chance for your business growth due to increased customer base.

Other utilities: You need to consider other utilities like electricity and telephone system, and the cost of electricity and telephones services should be reasonable. Determining the cost of electricity all includes the operations, installation process, fuel consumption, and greenhouse type.

Rules and regulations: Before running any greenhouse, you need to get approval from the Federal, state, and local governments. You should also check building and wetlands regulations and get a license to operate the greenhouse. Different regulations apply to different countries, so make sure to do enough research based on the laws for that country.

Types of Greenhouses

The type of greenhouse structure determines the productivity and efficiency of your gardening activities. New to greenhouse gardening? Don't you worry—this section will examine the different greenhouse designs and highlight the advantages and disadvantages of each structure. It will make it easier for beginners to choose the right structure based on their needs.

As a plant grower, you need to understand the efficiency of plant production and control of environmental conditions. Choosing the right greenhouse will enable you to create an ideal working environment for your vegetables, herbs, and fruits. It also allows you to create a plant growing plan that ensures you meet the specific needs of your crop.

These designs are based on the materials, shape, utility, and construction process. Most designs are classified as:

Attached

- Lean-to greenhouse structure
- Even span greenhouse structure

Freestanding or independent structures

- Uneven span greenhouse structure
- A-frame greenhouse structure
- Quonset greenhouse structure
- Gothic arch greenhouse structure

Gutter connected structures

- Ridge and furrow type greenhouse
- Sawtooth greenhouse

Lean-to Greenhouse Structure

Just like the name suggests, a lean-to greenhouse structure is built leaning on the side of another structure. It is classified as an **attached greenhouse structure**, meaning that the roof of the greenhouse connects to another building. You don't have to build all the four walls of the greenhouse because, by design, it shares one of its walls.

GREENHOUSE

Lean-to greenhouse structure

The structure should face the right direction to obtain adequate sunlight exposure. It should mostly face the southern side and the roof should have the best covering material. a lean-to greenhouse is ideal for growing herbs and vegetables.

This structure was common during the Victorian period, and it is one of the *traditional* structures available. Building against the wall offers additional support to the structure, making it strong and wind resistant. The wall also absorbs heat during the day and releases that heat at

GREENHOUSE

night, which helps to maintain the temperature of the greenhouse during the cool nights.

If you're planning to use lean-to structure, you need to put the height of the structure into consideration together with any metal base. This ensures the ridges do not come in contact with any windows or drainage pipes in the principal building.

Advantages

- *Cost-effective*: This type of structure is less expensive compared to other greenhouse structures.

- *Minimize building materials*: The design is built against an existing wall, thus saving you on building material for four walls. It also minimizes roofing material requirements, since the design makes the best use of sunlight.

- The structure is constructed close to water, electricity, and heat.

Disadvantages

- *Limited sunlight*: Building lean-to structure against a house or garage limits the amount of sunlight to only the three walls. It will also have limited light, ventilation, and minimum temperature control.

- *Limited to the building orientation:* The best structure should be on the southern exposure. The height of the building or the supporting wall affects the design and the size of the greenhouse.

- *Temperature control:* It is difficult to control the temperature of the structure because the wall absorbs a lot of heat during the day and distributes it for use in the cool nights. Some translucent covers lose heat more rapidly, making it difficult to control the heat.

- *Foundation:* You need to build a strong foundation for this greenhouse to last long, especially when using glass with the lean-to greenhouse.

Even Span Greenhouse Structure

Even span is another attached type of greenhouse, and it attaches more to promote plant growth. This standard structure is attached to a building, and its roof is made of two slopes of equal length and width. The structure can allow you to plant two to three rows, with two side benches and a wide bench at the center.

Even span design is more flexible and has curved eaves to boost their shape. Due to its great shape, there is

GREENHOUSE

plenty of air circulation in the greenhouse, thus making it easier to control temperatures. You also need to have an extra heating system especially when the structure is far away from a heated building. The heating system is especially important during the winter season.

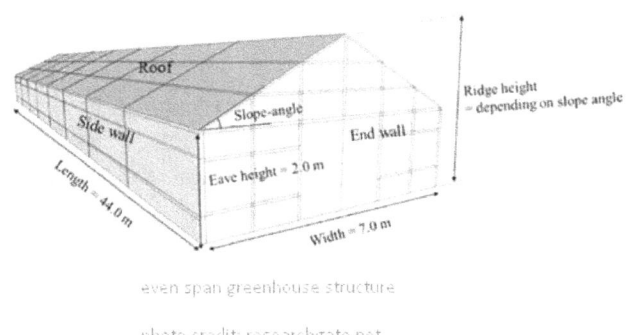

even span greenhouse structure

photo credit: researchgate.net

Advantages

- It provides enough space for the growth of plants and vegetables.

- It is easier and more economic in construction, making it the most popular design for a greenhouse.

- You have easy access to water and electricity within the building.

Disadvantages

- High cost of construction and heating system compared to the lean-to structure.

- Reduced sunlight exposure due to the shadow from the house it is attached to.

Uneven Span Greenhouse Structure

In this structure, the roof is made of uneven or unequal width. The greenhouse is constructed such that one rooftop slope is longer than the other, making the design suitable for a hilly terrain or when you want to take advantage of solar energy.

Uneven slopes are laid so the steeper angles of the greenhouse face to the south. The transparent section should face south, whereas the opaque side of the greenhouse should face north to conserve energy.

Uneven greenhouses are no longer used because most farmers prefer setting up a greenhouse on a flat land.

GREENHOUSE

Uneven-span greenhouse structure
Photo credit pinterest

Advantages

- As mentioned, this greenhouse is in a hilly areas.

- There is no obstruction of sunlight because the longer slope allows for more sunlight to enter the structure. The longer side also faces south, thus maximizing heat from the sun's rays.

Disadvantages

- It can be costly compared to even span greenhouses.

- They require more support on the slanted roof.

- Uneven span greenhouses usually need a lot of maintenance on the roof after some time.

- Too much solar can penetrate to the greenhouse if the uneven-span greenhouse is located in areas close to the equator.

A-Frame Greenhouse Structure

The A-frame greenhouse style is one of the most common designs. The structure is simple to set and it is ideal for a small backyard garden. To form the A-frame, you would attach the roof and sidewalls of greenhouse together, which forms a triangular-like shape.

GREENHOUSE

Most of A-framed greenhouses use translucent, polycarbonate material, which helps to eliminate the cost from having to buy glass material. Most A-framed greenhouses are laid down in an open field or at the backyard facing the southern side.

Advantages

- It maximizes on the use of space along the side walls.

- Simple and straightforward to construct.

- Conservative structure style, using minimal material.

- *Disadvantages*

- It has poor air circulation at the corners of the triangle.

- Its narrow side walls limit the overall use of the greenhouse.

Quonset Greenhouse Structure/ Hoop-House Structure

GREENHOUSE

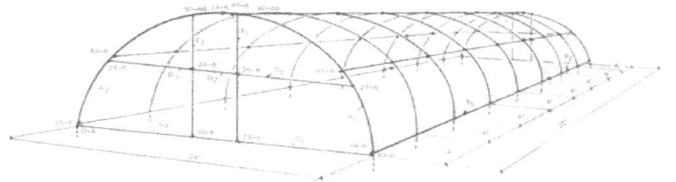

The quonset design has a curved roof or arched rafters, and its design is similar to military-hut style. The circular band in the structure's style is made of aluminum or PVC pipes, while the rooftop is made of plastic sheeting. The sidewalls of the design are set low, however, so there is not a whole lot of headroom. The hoops on the rooftop ensure there is no accumulation of snow and water on the top.

You would build this type of greenhouse in an open field or backyard with the structure facing the southern side.

Advantages

- Easy to build and one of the cheapest designs due to the use of plastic sheeting.

- Its design allows rain water and melted snow to run off.

- Suitable for a small plant growing space.

Disadvantages

- Limited storage space.
- Its frame design is not as sturdy as A-frame design.
- As stated, there is less headroom in the structure.

Gothic Arch Greenhouse Structure

Gothic arch has a nice aesthetic, and is one of the most visually pleasing designs available. The walls of the structure are bent over a frame, forming a pointed roof-like structure. The design requires less material to construct, as there is no need for trusses. Most of Gothic arch designs are made of plastic sheeting, and its design allows you to construct a large greenhouse where you can plant various products in rows.

Advantages

- The design has minimum heat exposure, thus making it easy to conserve heat.

- Plastic sheeting reduces the cost of construction.

- It has a simple and efficient design that allows rainwater and snow to flow away.

Disadvantages

- Not enough headroom and the design has a low sidewall height, which limits the storage of the greenhouse design.

Ridge and Furrow Greenhouse Structure

GREENHOUSE

This type of design uses two or more A-framed design structures connected to one another along the roof eave length. The eaves offer more protection and act as a furrow to allow melted snow or rain water to flow away.

There are no side walls on the structure, which creates more ventilation in the greenhouse. It also reduces automation cost and fuel consumption, since only small wall area is exposed where the heat can escape.

Ridge and furrow greenhouse structure is ideal for growing vegetables, and they're mostly used in Europe, Canada, the Netherlands, and Scandinavian countries.

GREENHOUSE

Advantages

- Ideal for large scale farming, and it's easy to expand this type of greenhouse.

- Provides more ventilation into the greenhouse.

- Requires few materials for construction because of its lack of side walls.

- Requires little energy to cool and heat.

Disadvantages

- Lack of proper water drainage system will damage your plants.

- Although the design has no side walls, shadows from the gutters can prevent sunlight from entering the greenhouse.

Sawtooth Greenhouse Structure

GREENHOUSE

This type of greenhouse structure is similar to the ridge and furrow; however, sawtooth offers more natural ventilation. This is due to its natural ventilation flow path developed as a result of the sawtooth design. The roof provides 25% of the total ventilation to the greenhouse, and opening the sawtooth vents will ensure there is continuous airflow into the greenhouse. This makes it easy to control the temperatures and ensure the plants are in good climatic conditions for their growth.

Advantages

- Sawtooth arches provide excellent light transmission into the greenhouse.

- High rooftop allows for natural heat ventilation and airflow in the greenhouse.

- Excellent structure for both warm and cold climatic conditions.

- Simple and strong greenhouse structure.

- Has a large farming area.

Cold Frame Greenhouse Structure

Cold frame is ideal for greenhouse gardening in your backyard, and allows you to plant plants and vegetables at any time. It is one of the cheapest and simplest greenhouses you can set up. In cold frame gardening, you place a glass or plastic sheeting as the cover of the greenhouse structure, which will help in protecting your crops from frost, snow, rain, wind, or low temperatures.

Cold-frame greenhouse is suitable for planting cold-loving plants like broccoli, cauliflower, and cabbage among others.

Based on your budget, you can go for glass, polycarbonate, or plastic sheeting material to construct the greenhouse. The design requires a few openings to allow ventilation of heat into the greenhouse.

Advantages

- Simple design and easy to manage.
- Made from old windows or old wood pallets, which minimizes the cost of construction.

Disadvantages

- Overheating problem—a single day with a lot of sun and closed windows can do a lot of damage to the plants.
- Recycling of the old materials can affect the material quality of the greenhouse.

Hotbed Greenhouse

The hotbed structure acts as a miniature type of greenhouse that traps heat from solar radiation. This greenhouse can provide a favorable environment for plants that need a lot of heat like tomatoes, eggplants, and peppers.

If you want to extend the growing season, you can use hotbeds to provide the right weather conditions for your crops. Whether during winter, summer, or spring, there is always a family of vegetables, fruits, or herbs you can grow.

The hotbed structure provides a heat source to the crops through manure rather than using heat source from electricity, helping to speed up the growth of your plants.

When using a hotbed, you can set up the garden as wide as you want, provided the ratio of manure used and the growing medium is 3:1. The amount of time and money you invest in the garden will determine your farm produce success.

Advantages

- Simple to design.
- Inexpensive.

Disadvantages

- Hotbeds only lasts two months, so you will need to remove and replace the material with new ones around that time.

Window Farm

GREENHOUSE

A window farm is an indoor farming garden for most vegetables. In a window farm, plants rely on the natural light from the window and temperature control from your living area to grow. This method is ideal for those who don't have a backyard or enough space to construct a standalone greenhouse.

You should set the structure in a window where it can receive a lot of light, facing toward the south.

Advantages

- Amazing for growing vegetables.
- Simple design and easy to construct.

Disadvantages

- Requires more components like nutrients, tubes, and pumps to grow your vegetables.
- It is difficult to maintain compared to a normal, soil-based greenhouse.

Construction of the Greenhouse

When building a greenhouse, you have to pay close

attention to its base. Ensure you have a secure base and that it's leveled up. Most structures have a metal base designed from a metal frame, which is separate from the rest of the structure.

You need to secure the base on the ground to avoid any movement. Make sure it's strong enough to withstand heavy winds, as such an event could be disastrous.

Site planning for where to layout the greenhouse is important too, and you should also evaluate the soil. Depending on the soil underneath, you can prepare your soil structure and texture. For example, if the soil is light and sandy, you have to install concrete or use slabs in the area.

GREENHOUSE

Types of Greenhouse Foundations

Soil/Earth Base

If the selected site has firm soil, construct concrete walls at the four corners of the frame. Level up the base of the structure before setting in the concrete walls. If the area has a slope, you need to use more soil to level up and firmly compact it down using rollers or with a vibrating plate.

Creating a soil base greenhouse allows you to cultivate fruits and vegetables directly in the soil. You can also be assured of good drainage. A soil base greenhouse

GREENHOUSE

foundation is one of the cheapest methods for constructing a greenhouse; although, there is a possibility of the frames subsiding, leading the breakage on the glass material.

If the soil drains poorly, the greenhouse can become muddy and waterlogged, which can allow for rodents and pests to breed inside.

Perimeter Base

You can create a perimeter base for the greenhouse, which you can make from slabs, concrete material, or breeze blocks. Measure the size of the base, then mark it with spray paint. Firmly fix the slabs or blocks down with a mixture of cement.

You can dig the area you want to fix to ensure you have a strong foundation. Laying the base directly on the sand can make the greenhouse unstable.

This kind of base provides you with a solid and cost-effective structure for building the greenhouse.

Slabs or Paving Base

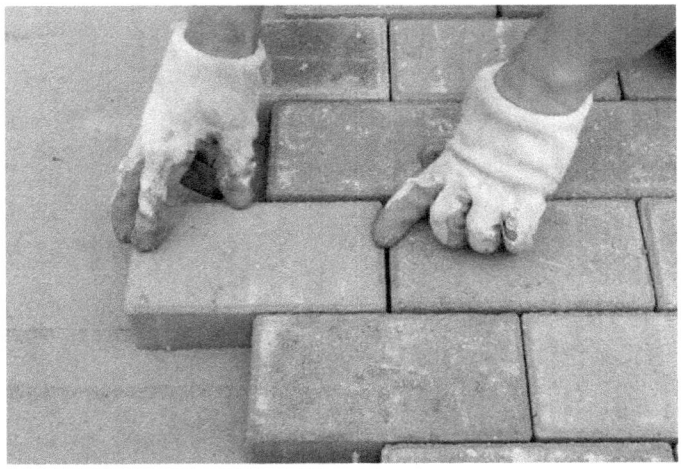

If you're looking for aesthetic, then you should use a slabs base. Having this type of base makes it easy to maintain the greenhouse, and you can plant your vegetables and fruits on the growing bags, containers, or pots.

This type of base is long-lasting and firmly fixed on the ground with the use of heavy duty plugs and multiple screws.

You can easily reorganize your greenhouse and keep it clean with this base. Water will be able to drain easily via the cracks on the slabs, though growing plants will be limited to using growing pots, bags, and containers.

It is the most expensive compared to perimeter and soil base.

Concrete Base

GREENHOUSE

A concrete base is suitable if you plan to build a large greenhouse, as it makes it easy to raise the base level. Concrete base has a durable foundation and you can easily clean the base using a detergent soap and water, or by simply sweeping the area with a broom. Washing this base with detergents can also help keep diseases away from the greenhouse.

Make sure to drill holes on the concrete to allow proper drainage of water in the greenhouse.

Once you have the base set up, you can construct the type of greenhouse style and start growing your plants.

Layout of the Greenhouse Site

Using what you now know about the various greenhouse styles, you can choose the right one based on your needs and come up with the site layout for your garden. Follow through this guide to know how to set up a layout for your garden.

Set-up greenhouse plan: You need to come up with a master plan for constructing buildings or facilities within the site. The plan should show detailed information on existing facilities within the site, evaluate any constraints and benefits of the site, and determine where to construct a new facility.

A good plan will outline where to construct the greenhouse, where to build a storage area, and the headhouse. If you're planning to have an outdoor production, then the area you select should be only a few meters away, which will make shipping and moving the crops easier.

A headhouse is building that attaches to the greenhouse, or is a converted section in the greenhouse that acts as a working area, office, utility room, or a transplanting area.

You should plan for the expansion space. You can start out small at first, but as your business grows, you may want to expand the greenhouse; therefore, it is important to factor in expansion space in your master plan. Once you are satisfied with the plan, you can go ahead and look at other factors.

Parking area and access to facilities: If you're setting up a commercial greenhouse facility, you need to ensure employees can conveniently access the growing area by providing a good parking area. Ensure the site has enough parking space for loading vehicles within the storage buildings and growing area, and employees and customers should also have their own parking lot. You will need to build all driveways and parking areas sloping to provide proper drainage. Alternatively, you can use underground piping to carry the water away.

Storage area: An indoor storage area is essential to store the harvested crops before shipping and transportation to the retail market. You also need a storage area for all farm equipment, containers, and chemicals, which can either be a separate building or in a headhouse. An outdoor storage area can be used for growing mix.

Outdoor facilities: You can set up an outdoor production facility to act as the growing bed or a shade house. The structure should have adequate lighting, a good drainage system, and an adequate water supply. The production area should be in a rectangular shape measuring about 1000 to 2000 square feet.

GREENHOUSE

Chapter Summary

The key to successful gardening is meeting all the requirements for your garden. You also have to come up with site layout that will guide you in planning all your gardening facilities. Greenhouse gardening can help you maximize your crop production. A well-designed greenhouse will ensure there is maximum space utilization and enable you to accurately control temperature conditions.

The right greenhouse structure is one that will last you a long time. Choose a design that meets your demands and fits in your budget. Once satisfied with a particular type of greenhouse design, you should learn more on how to utilize the greenhouse to grow the best produce.

The foundation of the structure chosen also contributes to the success of the greenhouse. Choosing a long-lasting base structure will help you set up a strong greenhouse structure with less maintenance. The base structure will determine the drainage system in the area and help you better understand the soil you need in your garden.

Growing vegetables or herbs in the greenhouse allows you to control the climate conditions within the growing environment and any other external constraints. To yield maximum benefit, you need a tailor-made greenhouse that helps you increase produce for your vegetables, fruits, and herbs. Always remember that what has worked for someone else may not work for you or meet your own requirements; therefore, you should start small and grow your garden with time.

In the next chapter, you will learn how various climatic conditions may affect your greenhouse garden.

CHAPTER TWO

OPERATING A GREENHOUSE

Growing the plants in the greenhouse can be your ultimate dream; however, there is more to greenhouse than just setting up the structure. You need to know how to maintain the greenhouse and ensure there is optimum conditions for the plants to thrive.

Having your own greenhouse will enable you to grow vegetables all year round, exotic plants, or herbs, and start the seeding process early. There are many reasons why you should set up your own greenhouse garden.

From the previous chapter, you learned that greenhouses come in a variety of styles and designs, ranging from a simple framed structure to full-size glass construction. Depending on your needs, you can purchase or build your own structure.

Each greenhouse model includes some temperature control features and other components to help you utilize the greenhouse's functions. Some of these components or amenities include electricity, heat, water, lighting, shelves, and benches. For example, the heating system enables you to grow your plants anytime of the year, so you don't have to worry about which season is the best for growing each crop. The lighting will enable you walk into the garden, even in the dark, and work on the crops, including planting new ones, trimming, and cutting.

Controlling Temperature Conditions

Controlling the temperatures within the greenhouse is essential for your crops' survival. Let's look at each of the following conditions and how you can regulate them and maximize on your produce.

Heating

Once you set up the greenhouse, you need to keep the temperature of greenhouse between 80° to 85°F (27° to 29°C). During the day, the greenhouse harnesses heat energy from the sun's rays and uses it to heat the internal air inside the garden. You can also get heat from other sources like electric heaters or gas.

A hot water boiler is highly recommended as a heating system. Water temperature should be regulated to satisfy the needs of each heating system. Depending on the specific crop's needs, each greenhouse should have independent temperature control.

Any of these heat sources can quickly heat up the structure to higher temperatures of over 100°F (40°C), which can kill your crops. Therefore, you need to regulate the interior temperature to a range of 80° to 85°F (27° to 30°C).

Ventilation and Air Flow

When designing a greenhouse, you must include vents either at the rooftop that with a hatch you can open on the ceiling, or have side vents. Plants need carbon dioxide (CO_2) to grow and release oxygen (O_2) and moisture into the environment. You need good ventilation in the area to avoid growing the crops under humid conditions.

Fans will be a great addition for cooling the environment, as they can whisk out the hot air and introduce a cooler air inside. You can choose to operate the vents either manually or automatically. If you install manual vents, make sure you open them every day and close them at night.

If you're on a budget, the manual vent system can work for you as long as you will always be available to open and close it as the weather changes. If you're not always around, maintaining a manual vent system may be difficult for you; therefore, an automated system would be the best alternative.

An automatic ventilation system uses a sensor programmed to automatically turn on the fans or the heating system when temperatures change. The sensors monitor temperatures when they rise and fall and automatically switch the fans and heaters on or off. This ensures constant air circulation and cooling of the greenhouse structure.

During the warmer days, you can ensure there is enough ventilation by opening the door to your garden. Make sure to put a heavy rock on the door or tie it to prevent wind from shutting it. If the structure is made of cold frames, you can also open the lid to allow more air to circulate inside during the day.

Lighting

To control the light levels, you need to have a shade cloth in either green or any other dark color. You can place the material on all the windows on the outside of the greenhouse, and you can roll it up and down to adjust the temperatures inside the greenhouse. This material will act as a shade and can prevent an excess of light from entering through the windows.

The shade cloth is crucial during the summer months. It helps in regulating heat and cooling the greenhouse temperatures, while allowing moderate light inside the structure. During the winter months, you can roll the cloth up to allow more light to enter inside.

Humidity

The amount of humidity present in your garden is essential in determining your vegetables' survival. You must keep the garden environment humid at all times, and at least ensure you have a humidity of 50% or higher.

The best strategies for adding more humidity to your crops is through:

- Taking a tray of pebbles and placing it under your crops.

- Covering the pebbles with water and putting them near the crops. As the water in the pebbles evaporates, it adds more humidity in the air.

- Placing stone chips or marbles under the crop benches or on a table. These stone chips may add more humidity to the crops, especially when placed on a dry day.

Benches are great for keeping moisture away. A **bench** is a type of table that has lips at the edge, and it is used to hold plants in place. Wooden benches have a tray inserted on it to keep moisture away from the wood, whereas metal benches have a mesh top attached to them to make it easy drain water and moisture.

How to Keep the Greenhouse Warm

1. Using Bubble Wrap to Insulate the Greenhouse

Insulating a greenhouse garden with a bubble wrap will ensure heat doesn't escape away. For a better insulation, buy a wrap with bigger bubbles. You should also cover all doors and windows to ensure heat doesn't escape, especially during the winter. This practice will not only keep the greenhouse warm, but it will also reduce the cost of heating.

2. *Using Heaters*

A small heater added to the greenhouse can help regulate the greenhouse's temperature, especially during the night. The plants can use the carbon dioxide produced by the heater and convert it to oxygen, which is essential for humans.

The cold weather outside will not be able to affect your plants inside the greenhouse if you have a heater installed.

3. *Using Air Circulators Inside the Greenhouse*

Heaters will not be enough to provide warmth inside the greenhouse; you will also have to make sure the fresh air being circulated inside the greenhouse is warmed evenly to avoid having cold and hot patches on the plants.

Installing air circulators will ensure there is an even distribution of warm air inside the greenhouse. You can buy an air circulator fan or use the air circulation function from KlimaHeat to mix air.

If you have no electricity in the area, you can protect the plants from the cold weather by:

1. *Using Compost*

The bacteria that breaks down organic matter during the compost process generates heat; therefore, adding more compost to the soil will help generate heat that can keep your plants warm.

Add a layer of soil about 3 inches thick to enable the bacteria to create a warm environment for the plant roots.

2. Using a Double Layer of Plastic Material to Make Windows

Insulating the windows can help the greenhouse retain more heat. Although insulation can block the amount of light from entering, using a double layer of insulation material on the windows can add more warmth inside. As a result, you double the R-value (insulation) of the greenhouse.

3. Using Black Mulch on All Pathways

The pathways inside the greenhouse or between the planting beds absorb heat. Adding black mulch, or any other dark color mulch, to the pathways will absorb more sunlight and convert it to heat, keeping your plants' roots warm.

4. Using Heat to Absorb Barrels

Put black barrels in an area where they can have direct access to sunlight, as they will absorb more sunlight and use that to convert heat that will warm the water inside. As it goes, you should place the plastic black barrels in water.

The warm water created will act as thermal mass and can hold for a longer period, providing warmth to greenhouse plants.

Although they use sunlight themselves, make sure to place the barrels in a way that they won't block sunlight from reaching the plants. Barrels work well when placed on the northern corner of the greenhouse. During the summer, you should cover these barrels with a white material to prevent them from creating extra heat in the greenhouse.

5. Building the Greenhouse Partially Underground

Building the greenhouse 4 inches deeper on the ground will help retain more warmth and acts as an insulator against the cold air from outside the structure. During the cold season, the ground will be warm. This provides the warmth needed for the roots of the plant to grow.

If you have a greenhouse building facing the south hillside, it will absorb more heat to warm the ground.

6. Utilizing Thermal Mass Objects

Using objects like clay, rocks, and bricks can absorb heat when the air circulating inside is warm and release the absorbed heat when the air inside is cold. Therefore, having raised beds made of clay or brick material can absorb heat and use it to warm the greenhouse. You can boost the amount of warmth released by adding black barrel to water inside.

7. *Insulating the Northern Side*

If you stay in Northern hemisphere, there is no need to fix glass on the northern side because the sun doesn't shine on that side. Adding insulators on the northern side will help retain heat inside the greenhouse and prevent north winds from getting inside. In addition, putting a thermal heating mass on the wall can absorb more sunlight.

Chapter Summary

Greenhouses need to be set to optimum conditions for the plants to thrive. Building your own greenhouse allows you to adjust climatic condition to match the one suitable for the growth of plants and extend the growing season, meaning you won't have to stick to growing plants during the warm weather. Using a greenhouse, you can grow all-year round plants and have a constant supply of fresh food from your firm.

Both fruits, vegetables, and herbs require different climatic conditions, and depending on your location, you can adjust greenhouse temperatures, lighting, and humidity to match your crop needs.

You have to install vents and fans in the greenhouse to ensure there is fresh air circulation in the structure and make the conditions unfavorable for breeding of pests and diseases.

To maximize the plants' yields, you need to maintain a good growing environment and ensure the greenhouse is kept warm at all times. There are various tools you can use to ensure the greenhouse stays warm or utilize non-electrical methods to keep the structure warm.

In the next chapter, you will learn about various tools and equipment essential for running a greenhouse.

CHAPTER THREE

GREENHOUSE EQUIPMENT

Having the best greenhouse equipment is crucial for efficiently managing your greenhouse. The equipment will help in your operation, maintenance, and improvement of the greenhouse, and there is a wide variety of equipment and other accessories for all your greenhouse in the market.

The choice of equipment to use depends on the types of crops and the climatic conditions of the area. That is, are you located in an area that experience heavy snow and with a lot of wind, or are you in an area that experiences extreme heat or cold? This information is important when buying greenhouse equipment.

The equipment used only for raising seedling will be different to those you would use for full cycle planting fruits or vegetables. Your choice of the equipment and other accessories will ensure your ability to produce high quality crops and maintain an active produce for all-year round crops. You should keep the greenhouse structure warm and properly managed to create more space for plant germination.

Depending on the type of crop, planting can be on the floor or on the benches. A fixed peninsula and movable benches are highly recommended, as they help in creating more growing space. Other equipment like overhead conveyor trolleys and carts can contribute to reduced cost of material handling.

Basic Equipment

When you think of starting your own greenhouse garden, there are basic considerations you need to think about, such as where to get the seeds, pots, and trays to plant your crops.

The choice of these greenhouse containers will have an impact on how the vegetables, herbs, and the fruits grow.

The containers you use in the garden should be able to grip the soil and promote good health to the seeds. They should also offer enough room for the roots to grow and provide an excellent drainage system. This ensures the crops are in good condition and promote their growth.

Containers can hold several planting trays and pots to provide crop growth and stability, and as a result, there will be an upward growth to your crops. These containers can be in the form of plugs, flats, pots, and hanging baskets. A larger container can fit several pots inside and provide enough space to grow the seeds.

Hanging baskets are great for planting your vegetables and herbs in the garden. There are plenty of these baskets in the market, and they will provide enough space for your crops' growth. Most of the baskets will be plastic or coconut fiber, while others will be made of ceramic metal. You can buy any material based on your budget.

You would use **flats** and **plugs** during the *germination stage*. They ensure the vegetables grow separately and keep your garden neat.

Most gardeners prefer pots made of **clay**, as they give the growing of plants like fruits, flowers, and vegetables a more traditional look. If you're on a budget, you can buy **plastic pots** or **wood pots**, which are more durable and cheaper. You can dispose of plastic and wood pots much easier than clay pots.

You can also consider the use of seed boxes to help you in the germination of the seeds. The boxes can be made of plastic or wood material and they provide you with excellent space to grow your fruits and vegetables.

How to Choose Good Containers and Pots

If you're using **porous containers**, you will find that you have to continue watering the crops, as the soil dries out very quickly. This can lead to wasting water and increase the cost of water. In **non-porous containers**, you use less water because the soil grips moisture, thus, retaining enough water content for a day.

Therefore, when choosing any of those containers discussed above, they should not only satisfy the growth of crops but also provide enough drainage and porosity.

Mobility of the pots and containers is also important, especially if plan to have all-year-round crops in the garden. They should be made of lightweight material to make it easy to move them around.

Choosing the right container will contribute significantly to the growth of vegetables, herbs, and fruits in your greenhouse.

Furniture to Store Greenhouse Equipment

Shelves: You need a furniture that will help you arrange all the containers and provide adequate **shelving** in the greenhouse. If you have a small space in the greenhouse, you can use shelves to boost on the growing space.

GREENHOUSE

There are movable greenhouse shelves that you can move out and back inside during favorable climatic conditions.

Always remember that **double shelving** can affect the amount of lighting required by the crops.

You can build temporary shelves or have permanent shelves attached to the structure to start your seedlings. You can also have shelves built beneath the garden benches to help you create more space in the greenhouse.

You can build shelves made of wood, glass, or metal. The wire mesh you use in building the shelves helps in draining the excess water from the crops.

Another important reason for creating shelves is to ensure all the crops are separate from one another to avoid **cross-pollination**. Depending on the size of the shelves, it can store more pots and containers.

Garden benches: Another furniture inside the greenhouse are **garden benches**. The greenhouse structure determines the size of the benches in the garden, and these benches can be temporary or permanently built. Installing benches is great for optimizing the growing space in the garden, and section benches are ideal for regular movement and creating new plant arrangements.

Planters: These are widely common in today's modern

greenhouse gardens. The long and deep **planters** are highly recommended for growing fruits, vegetables, or any other food crops. The planters are designed in such a way that each can only hold a single vegetable or fruit plant.

Lighting System Equipment

The amount of light inside the greenhouse determines the level of sunlight in the greenhouse. If the amount of sunlight in the greenhouse is not strong enough, you can supplement it with artificial light.

Before choosing the lighting system to use for boosting plant growth, you need to determine the amount of solar radiation available in that area, as that will affect the amount of light needed for photosynthesis.

Others factors you need to look at is the size and type of greenhouse structure. You also need to consider the crops growing, as some of them require high-intensity light, while others will do better in low light or shade.

You should consider the space available for hanging the lighting system, and it should be easy to adjust based on the crops' needs. For example, as some plants, like fruits, increase in height as they grow, the lighting system should be moved upwards. Therefore, you need to factor in the wiring system and the socket space.

Some of the tools for providing artificial light include:

Light intensity meter: This instrument has an installed universal-sensor probe that measures the intensity of light at any angle. The equipment monitor can maintain an ideal growing light for all plants in the garden.

Grow lights: Grow lights are excellent for providing a cool and warm light for the growth of house plants, herbs, and fruits. The grow lights act as a replacement of sunlight when growing plants indoors. There are different types of grow lights in the market to choose from, such as fluorescent, LEDs, high pressure sodium, among others.

Seedling lights: As the seeds germinate, they require a lot of light; therefore, you need to place them in an area where they can have a maximum access to light. Each plant grown requires a different light intensity, and most plants in a greenhouse garden require a high light intensity to flourish. You can have fluorescent bulbs installed in the garden to provide maximum light to all your crops.

High Intensity Discharge lamp (HID): If you have a large greenhouse structure with big plants like fruits and flowers, you need to install HID lamps. These lamps emit more light compared to other types of lights, boosting plant growth. The lamp fixtures have reflectors fitted on it to reflect the light back to the crops.

GREENHOUSE

This type of lamp produces a lot of heat, so you should keep it far away from the plants to avoid burning their leaves.

LED Lights: LED lights are suitable for vegetables and herbs. They're the best greenhouse lights and the most efficient for quick plant growth. The lights are long-lasting and easy to install.

Temperature Control and Heating System Equipment

To control the temperature, you need to install an **electronic controller** in the garden. This control will monitor and manage the temperatures of the heating system and ventilation equipment.

Thermostats: If you have a small greenhouse garden, you can use thermostats that record accurate temperatures within the garden, and they automatically control the temperature in a specific area. Make sure it is installed based on the plant height as this will make it easy to capture accurate readings on temperature conditions.

Thermometer: A thermometer measures the maximum and minimum temperature inside the garden and monitors any temperature changes. It helps in maintaining perfect temperatures for the growth of plants.

When buying thermometer for the greenhouse, look for one that is reset by a magnet. Although there are other types, the one with a magnet is highly recommended for greenhouses.

Hot air furnace or unit heaters: The unit heater is suitable when the greenhouse is shutdown during the winter season to drain water system. Installing unit heaters is one of the best decisions you can make for your crop production, as they control the temperature inside the greenhouse.

There are different types of heaters and based on your garden needs, such as gas, electric, or propane. You can also choose to use **vented** on **non-vented** heaters.

EPDM tubing: Temperature control on the benches or floor is also important. You can place the EPDM tubing on the concrete floor or in a sand layer to provide floor heating. If you plant your crops on the benches, you can place the EPDM tubing on the bench or use a low output radiation pin, which you would place under the bench to keep the area warm.

Hot water boiler: A hot water boiler is the best for maintaining the heating system. Make sure the water temperatures don't go beyond 75°F (24°C). The root zone heat provides the uniform temperatures of 70°F to 75°F (21°C to 24°C), which is essential for all plant growth. Root zone heat provides 25% of the heat needed for the coldest nights, while the remaining 75% heat comes from heat exchangers or a radiation pin installed under the gutters or around the perimeter of the greenhouse.

Humidistat: A humidistat equipment is needed to control moisture or humidity within the greenhouse.

In a large scale operation, you can easily integrate computer controls in the ventilation, lighting, and heating systems. Using computer-controlled systems ensures automatic control of environmental conditions within the greenhouse.

Ventilation Equipment

A proper ventilation system contributes to the growth of your plants. Sunlight changes throughout the year can cause temperature changes in the garden, so you need to have a good venting system installed to control the temperatures.

Vents: You can install vents on the roof or on the sides of the structure. Rooftop vents are the most common and one of the best venting systems.

If you're not around throughout the day, an automatic venting system will be ideal for you.

Exhaust fans: You would use exhaust fans to whisk away excess air and ensure there is a constant supply of fresh air inside.

Water Management Equipment Irrigation Equipment

If you're using plug trays with small cells for growing the crops, then you should have a programmed computer irrigation system to water different section of crops at different rates. Automating the watering system will make your work easier.

Customizing the watering system based on the individual needs of the crop bed ensures there is no overwatering or underwatering for each crop bed.

Plastic watering cans are highly recommended. They are cheap, lighter, and require less labor. However, if you want to maintain the beauty of the greenhouse, then you can use metal cans instead.

Another piece of equipment you can use is the **trickle watering system**. The trickle watering system uses a plastic horse with some outlet nozzles fitted at different intervals on the horse length.

You would place the horse pipes at proximity along the pots. Then, connect the horse to the water storage tank. You should fill the tanks with water consistently. Once full, it will release the water to all the crops.

The horse system will always water the pots and crop bed with a set water quantity and at the same time every day.

Other water equipment you will need in the garden include irrigation tubes, valves, water breakers, sprinklers, a hose, misters, and boilers. Boilers provide excellent temperature regulation.

Energy Conservation Equipment

Due to the high cost of fuel energy, coming up with energy conservation measures will help you reduce the cost of production. Some essential tools for energy conservation include perimeter insulation, energy screens or shades, and windbreakers.

Pest Control Equipment

Every greenhouse structure should have a pest control system. There are different methods you can use to control pests in the farm, some of which use chemicals while others use biological methods.

You can also use natural methods, like beneficial insects, to control pests.

Alternatively, you can use a metal, cloth, or thin plastic mesh to keep pests away from the garden. Fencing and use of door sweeps can also keep the bugs away from accessing specific planting sections.

Depending on which method to use, you can buy sprayers, fogging equipment, and formers.

You can also use insecticide and pesticide to protect vegetables and keep attacking bugs at bay.

Other Greenhouse Accessories

Soil Sterilizer

Although you may be considering using any of the available types of soil for potting the vegetables, you can also consider the use of **soil fertilizers**. There are various methods you can use to sterilize the soil, but the best method is using a **steam sterilization system**.

Installing a steam system is easy and cheap and ensures efficiency in your gardening.

Gardening Sieves

The soil texture is an important factor you have to consider in the seedling stage. It is important to ensure that you use the best texture for your baby plants to survive. A **sowing sieve** will help you achieve your goal by providing you with the desired texture for the baby plants.

You can also use a mesh sieve, which lightly covers the seeds with a compost once you plant them.

Plant Supporting Equipment

Sometimes, to increase your plants' strength and length, you can introduce the support equipment to provide adequate support to them as they grow. One way to provide support is by tying them together, so they can help hold each other up.

There are different materials you can use to tie the plants together, but you can try **raffia**, as it supports most of plants, and various stores sell it at a reasonable price.

To use raffia, you can soak it in water for a few hours before tying the plants with it. This practice helps avoid breakage and makes it stronger and more reliable.

GREENHOUSE

Chapter Summary

You need to keep your greenhouses warm and properly arranged to create more space for plant germination. Depending on the type of crop, planting can be on the floor or on the benches. A fixed peninsula and movable benches are highly recommended, as they help to add more growing space. Other equipment like overhead conveyor trolleys and carts can contribute to reduced cost of material handling.

You also need to install temperature control equipment to monitor the room temperature and adjust it based on the crops' needs.

The plants growing area should be well-ventilated to ensure the garden is free from any moisture or humid conditions, and there should be enough lighting to quicken the plants' growth. If the greenhouse is set in an area where there is no direct access to sunlight, you can use artificial lighting equipment as a supplement.

Other basic tools like benches and containers for seedlings are crucial for plant survival. All plants, no matter the method of plantation, require a good drainage system.

You need to maintain proper hygiene on all tools and accessories used in the greenhouse, which will help keep diseases at bay. You should set up a storage room too, either within the greenhouse or in a separate building, where you can store all these tools.

In the next chapter, you will learn how to cultivate fruit.

CHAPTER FOUR

CULTIVATING FRUITS

Fruits are excellent, healthy snacks for people, and are great in foods too. The nutrient value of fruits can motivate us to become fruit farmers to supply fresh fruits to a large community. However, growing your own fruit at home can be limited to the prevailing climatic conditions within the environment, and sometimes, the weather patterns are not suitable for certain types of fruits. In certain areas where there is a short growing season, or an area that faces a lot of winter cold and frost, greenhouses will be ideal for growing fruit.

Greenhouse gardens allow you to cultivate all kinds of fruit trees and control the greenhouse temperatures to ensure you can get a healthy harvest. You can grow some fruits all year round inside the greenhouse, while others may require you to move the fruit tree inside during the winter season.

GREENHOUSE

Whether you are setting up a home greenhouse or a commercial greenhouse, this tutorial will guide you on how to cultivate fruits.

You can plant fruit trees, vines, or shrubs in containers or pots. During the seedling stage, you should grow the fruits at low humidity levels to enable them thrive. Doing this also protects the fruits from pests and other diseases.

Greenhouse gardening opens doors to fruit diversification by allowing you to cultivate different types of fruits and employ different farming styles and techniques.

Some fruits like lemons, peaches, grapes, strawberries, and tomatoes are less demanding. Grapes need a cool growing environment to thrive, as water-logged soil can affect their vines. Therefore, you will need free-draining soil cultivate the fruit.

Young fruit trees require support to grow strong, and you can tie the fruit trees together to support each other.

Based on the fruit you want to cultivate, you can control the greenhouse temperature, light, humidity, and other factors to satisfy your crops climatic needs and boost their growth.

Most fruit trees thrive well in temperatures above 50°F (10°C). Other tropical fruit-trees like citrus require a temperature of 60°F (16°C).

Getting Started With the Seedling Stage

To start, you need to add the moist seed-starting mix to all the pots and seed starting trays. Then, plant the seeds in the pots based on the directions given on the seeds' packets. Most seed supplier companies recommend planting two to three seeds per pot. Once you have planted them, use soil to cover the seeds and water them with a good amount of water. Cover the pot or the seedling containers with a plastic wrap and place them in a brightly lit environment to speed up the seed growth. You should also monitor the temperature in the room to ensure it is conducive for the fruits growth.

You can invest in an electric heating mat, which will help in regulating the soil temperatures for the seeds' starting stage. Once the seeds germinate, you should remove the plastic wrap.

You should keep the planting mix moist at all times. Do not overwater the mix, as doing so may affect the plants' growth.

Using scissors, snip out excess seeding in the pot or container. Each pot should only have **one fruit tree** to grow well.

Adding Fertilizers

You should fertilize the fruit plant after every one or two weeks to keep the fruit tree's health optimal. Water each pot with ¼ cup of water soluble fertilizer, and do so after adding fertilizers to them.

After eight weeks, the fruit tree is ready to be transplanted to a larger container to continue growing, or planted outside if the climate is favorable for that type of fruit.

Always ensure proper maintenance of the greenhouse. You should put moisture retention mechanisms and free soil drainage practices to produce tasty fruits.

Soil Preparation

Soil preparation is an essential part of producing healthy fruits. There is nothing more satisfying than harvesting fresh, tasty fruits from your own backyard, which is the dream of every farmer. To get better results for your produce, it all begins from the soil preparation and planning.

Soil preparation involves coming up with a way to improve the soil you used for planting the fruits. This practice requires improving the soil nutrients, its composition, pH balance, soil consistency, and drainage.

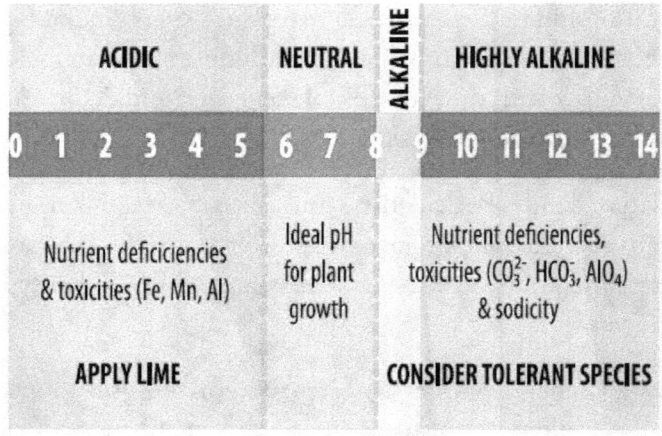

Proper preparation of the soil will ensure you harvest delicious and tasty fruits. The right type of soil should be able to increase the fruit production.

Fruit trees do well in soils with proper drainage and nutrients.

How to Improve Soil Drainage and Consistency

1. *Test Soil Drainage*

You can dig a hole in the planting area and fill it with water. The soil should be able to drain the water in three to four hours. Add more water and wait to drain it in three to four hours. If the water could not drain within that period, it is an indicator that the soil can't drain water enough and it *cannot* support the fruit tree's growth.

If it drains in less than three hours, the soil in that area is *sandy*. You can improve this by adding more organic matter into the soil.

You can improve soil drainage by building a drainage system, having raised beds in the greenhouse, or planting mounds.

2. Install a French Drainage System

If you're having a slow draining soil in the area, you can install French drains to speed up the drainage. Slow draining soil can be due to a thick and sticky clay layer clogging up underneath the topsoil. Installing the underground drainage pipes (French drainage system) can help solve the problem.

3. Use Organic Matter to Improve Soil Damage

If the soil is sandy and it rains quicker, the fruit trees may not get enough water to enable them grow healthy. You can solve this problem by adding a mix of composted organic matter to the soil. Doing this will help the soil to retain more moisture while the fruit tree roots are being established.

You can use a **rototiller** to mix the compost to the soil. You can buy or rent one from your local garden center.

After mixing the soil with organic matter, test it again with water and observe the drainage. As stated, it should drain within three to four hours.

The amount of organic matter added to the soil will depend on the rate of your soil drainage.

4. *Protect the Tree Root Crown with a Mound*

The root part of the fruit tree below the soil level is called the root crown. The **root crown** is vulnerable to excess moisture in the soil; therefore, you need to raise the planting area using a mound.

You can create a raised mound in your planting area by backfilling soil in the holes. This creates a gentle slope and raises the planting area, and the gentle slope prevents soil erosion.

5. *Build a Raised Bed to Protect the Root Crown*

You can also use raised beds instead to prevent soil erosion caused by the mounds.

You can build a raised bed through designing a simple wooden box, which will hold the soil around the fruit tree. The wooden box keeps the soil line raised high, and thus protecting the root crown from excess moisture.

6. Break Up the Soil Consistency for Better Root Growth

Tightly packed soil can limit the root growth. Fruit roots tend to do well in areas that are cultivated using shovels or rototiller, so you can use shovels to cultivate the planting area and break up the soil in that area.

Always make sure you don't cultivate below the recommended depth of planting fruit trees. If you notice the soil has a lot of clay as you cultivate, you can cut channels to create some holes. Doing this will prompt an outward root growth.

How to Test Soil Nutrients and pH

1. Use Soil Testing Kit

Nutrient soil testing kits are widely available. You can buy them from any hardware store or retailer like Home Depot, Walmart, or Target. The kit comes in different forms, and all of which will work for your needs. They test the soil and give results on its nutrients and pH level.

You can also send soil samples to the lab for further analysis. Some kits also provide home and lab testing; however, they are more expensive compared to other home testing kits.

2. Test Soil During Early Summer

Although you can test the soil at any time, choosing to test the soil in early summer or late spring will give you enough time to make adjustments to the soil before the next planting season. If you are in an area with different planting season, you can carry out testing at either the start of the growing season or at the end of the previous growing season.

Also note that the presence of moisture in the soil can give incorrect readings, so early tests may be more ideal.

3. *Clean the Testing Tools*

Before taking any soil samples, you need to clean the tools using mild soap and water. Make sure to properly rinse the soap well; otherwise, you will get a wrong reading. Use a paper towel to dry the tools, then you can test the sample taken.

4. *Take Soil Samples from the Planting Area*

When taking the soil samples, dig some holes spaced evenly from the planting area and take samples from each hole to test. Put all the samples in a dry, clean bucket and mix them well. After mixing, you can put them on dry newspaper to let them dry.

You can use a sample container packed with the testing kit to ensure you take an equal amount of sample soil from each hole.

Once the soil sample is dry, add the reagent to the

sample. As the soil reacts to the reagent, you should see the change in color, and you can read the result based on the pH level color chart provided in the kit.

How to Balance pH Level and Fertilize the Soil

From the provided pH level color chart, you can discern the type of soil you have, whether acidic or alkaline. Based on the results, you can decide to lower or increase the pH level, or whether to add more fertilizer to the soil to boost its nutrient value.

You can balance the pH by:

1. *Reducing Soil Acidity*

If the test shows the soil has high acidity, you need to reduce the excess acidity in the soil. One way of reducing the acidity level is to mix the soil with limestone. Make sure to follow the manufacturer's instructions for the quantity you should use for every mix.

You can add limestone each year at the beginning of every fall or during the summer. It may take some time before you can see the changes on the fruit's produce.

2. *Increasing the pH Level*

When the soil is alkaline, you can add some additives like

sulfur or gypsum to increase its pH. You can also apply compost material to the soil regularly to reduce its alkalinity.

Make sure to always test the soil every time you add compost; otherwise, you may make the soil too acidic.

3.   *Fertilizing the Fruit Tree*

Always add fertilizers to the fruit tree after planting. You should add the fertilizer at the top of the soil, mainly after the pruning process or before the budding of fruits.

Fruit roots are sensitive; therefore, you should avoid applying fertilizers or any manure directly to the hole where you will plant them.

4.   *Adding Nitrogen Fertilizer on the Fruit Tree*

Once the fruit tree has grown to be strong, you can add nitrogen light fertilizer. However, this practice will reduce fruit bearing wood, and you will have to trim a lot of overgrown branches or stems to encourage fruit growth.

As mentioned, if the soil has a more acidic pH, you can add more lime to the soil to raise its pH and make it more suitable for planting fruits. If the soil pH is not acidic enough, you can use sulfur to lower it.

Each soil additive has a different pH concentration, so always follow the manufacturer's instructions in each additive to adjust the pH level to where you need it to be.

You may note that, in most areas, clay soil has more nutrients and poor drainage. In such cases, you don't need to add more fertilizer to the soil—you only need to use compost manure to improve the soil drainage.

If you are cultivating fruits for commercial use, you can use potted fruit trees in a potting soil. You can create potting soil mixture by mixing equal proportions of peat, sand, and bark or perlite, and the mixture you use should have proper drainage. To boost the pot drainage, you can use a pot with large drainage holes. You can also place a layer of gravel at the bottom of the pot.

Water Requirements for Planting Fruits

Fruit trees require plenty of water for it to produce juicy fruit. The more water it receives, the juicier it will be. A young fruit tree will need a lot of water for its growth, which is especially true during hot and dry periods.

If the fruit doesn't receive enough water up to its roots end, it will develop a weak fruit tree with a shallow root system. Giving the right amount of water to the fruit tree is essential for producing a decent amount of fruits.

Watering Baby Fruit Trees

A newly planted fruit tree requires a lot of water to establish strong roots in the soil. Watering the fruit tree with plenty of water immediately after you plant it will enable the soil to remain moist and settle well around its root balls.

When the top soil starts to dry out, water the young fruit tree with more water. This will enable water to go in deep, and as a result, the fruit tree will have a healthier and deeper root system. Deep watering the fruit tree after every three days in the first two seasons will lead to a healthy and strong fruit tree.

Overwatering or **waterlogging** a young fruit tree in a pot can affect the root growth. Irregular watering can make some fruit trees bolt. which will result in growth of a poor and weak fruit tree.

Watering Mature Trees

Although mature trees require less water compared to baby trees, they regularly need a thorough watering to have juicy fruits. You can use drip irrigation to keep the soil moist and encourage a healthy root development. The tree will also be able to produce more juicy fruits.

Watering During Summer Periods

You need to keep the fruit tree soil moist and not waterlogged and continue watering the fruit tree until the harvest time. During the summer, water the fruit trees when at least 8 to 10 inches of the topsoil goes dry. Some fruit trees, like citrus, need to be watered when at least 3 to 4 inches of the top soil dries out.

During hot weather, you need to water them more often to ensure the fruit tree produces juicier fruits.

The amount of water needed depends on the fruit type, tree size, stage of growth, and temperature within the greenhouse or outdoors if transplanted outside. Fruits grown in sandy soil need watering almost daily during the summer because sandy soil does not retain water for long.

You may consider adding compost to the sandy soil to aid in retaining moisture. Alternatively, if you have planted the fruits on clay soil, you need to water the fruit tree more often. Be careful not to waterlog the tree, as clay soil is more prone to waterlogging.

To know how much water each fruit tree requires per day, you can use a **controlled drip irrigation**.

Drip irrigation helps in stabilizing the fruit tree's growth and maintains the quality of its fruit production. Water requirement is an important component for fruits grown in tropical and subtropical areas, and it determines the mass production of the fruit tree and the fruit quality.

Mulching the Fruit Tree

Farmers using a mulching process to improve the soil underneath. There are different materials you can use to improve the soil condition, and the type of material to use depends on the kind of soil in your garden.

You can apply a mulch to your fruit tree garden or even flower beds to grow a healthier fruit tree and keep away weeds or grass. Mulching makes the fruits drought resistant, as the practice helps the mulched soil retain more water. There will also be less weeding, watering, and even fewer pest problems.

Mulch can be in the form of wood chips or bark pieces, and you should pour natural mulch in circles to cover the whole root system. Mulching 3 to 4 inches deep discourages the growth of weeds around the fruit tree area. Apply mulch with care and do not cover the tree trunk or stems.

Sometimes, mulch can retain moisture. If that moisture piles up against the tree trunk or the stems, it can cause them to rot.

Why You Should Mulch Trees

- Helps in insulating the soil and protects the tree roots from heat and extreme cold.

- Helps retain water in the soil, and as a result, the roots can stay moist for longer.

- Enables you to create a stable, cool, and moist environment surrounding the root system.

- Protects the fruit tree from damage caused by lawnmowers.

- Reduces competition from the surrounding plants, such as grass and weeds.

How to Maintain Fruit Tree Health

During the first two years of planting the tree, you should give the fruit tree extra care by watering and fertilizing.

Always water the tree deeply at least twice or thrice per week to encourage deep root development. If you have planted the fruit tree in a rocky area with fast draining soil, you should water the tree root ball and the surrounding soil regularly.

You should also inspect the fruit tree often. Be sure to look at:

- **The leaf size of the fruit**—indicates any change.

- **New leaves or buds**—indicates change compared to previous buds or leaves.

- **Trunk decay or any deformation**—indicates stem decay or a problem that has been affecting the tree from a young age.

- **Curled leaves**—can indicate fungi or pest infection especially if on new leaves.

- Any twig growth.

Fruit Tree Pollination

Pollination is an important factor in fruit production process. Without pollination, your plants would produce few fruit. Pollination is the process of transferring pollen from the male parts to the stigma in the female parts of a plant. Most plants are either self-pollinators, or they rely on insect and wind pollinators.

Pollinators can transfer pollen either within the same flower or across flowers in different plant species.

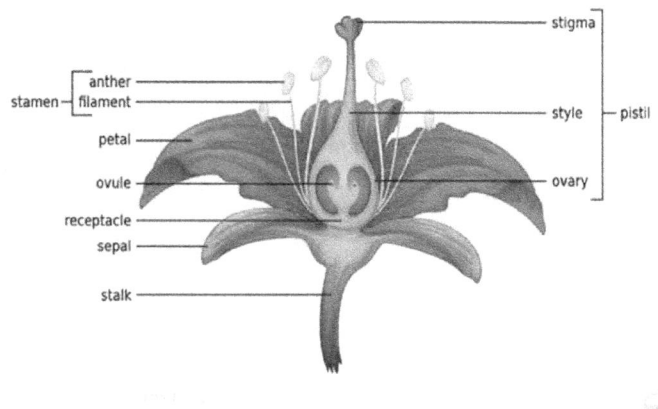

Fruit trees require pollination to produce fruits. The majority of fruit-tree species do not self-pollinate; therefore, they need pollinators to aid in the pollination process.

Pollination can either be:

- Wind or insect pollination
- Self-pollination by use of a pollen sprayer or hand pollination
- Cross pollination

In **cross pollination,** a plant pollinates another plant of different species to produce a **genetic plant**. Fruit tree cross pollination will produce a fruit with characteristics from two pollinating plants.

Fruits cross pollinated by insects produce more fruits than self-pollinated fruits, and bees are the main fruit tree pollinators.

Some plants that need insect pollinators to make the fruit juice include:

- Watermelons
- Apples
- Blackberries
- Blueberries
- Raspberries
- Pears
- Cucumber
- Plums

Other fruits are **self-pollinating** and do not require any other plants to pollinate their flowers. In this type of pollination, pollination occurs on the same flower.

Chapter Summary

Since fruits do well in cool, humid, and mild winters, growing them in a greenhouse will give them an

GREENHOUSE

adequate temperature to enhance their growth. You can also adjust the temperatures of the structure. The greenhouse can protect the fruit trees from wind damage too, especially citrus, which is a fruit that cannot tolerate the wind.

Planting free-standing fruits requires you to dig a large hole and add compost manure or horse manure to the soil and cover the mixture. Monitor the soil temperature and when the temperature drops to 85°F (29°C), then you can add seeds to the seedling trays.

Always monitor the temperature to ensure they don't drop 85°F (29°C).

The ideal soil for growing fruits should be well-drained with loam texture. Fruits also need a deep root system, so a deep soil with topsoil of at least 3 feet is highly recommended. You should also test the soil to know the type present in your garden or yard, so you can know the adjustments to make to the pH level and nutrient value of the soil. Most fruits need a 6 to 6.5 pH balance.

In the next chapter, you will learn how to cultivate vegetables.

CHAPTER FIVE

CULTIVATING VEGETABLES

Greenhouses are an ideal place to cultivate vegetables all year round. It allows you to start off the vegetable garden without waiting for a particular season. You can also harvest some vegetables early, such as French beans.

During the summer months, you can grow vegetables like cucumbers, tomatoes, peppers, and chillies. Some of these vegetables are low maintenance and easy to plant in your backyard.

Greenhouses provide you with a controlled environment where you can try other heat-loving vegetables like sweet potatoes, okra, and melons. You don't have to worry about the climatic conditions of your location—with the various greenhouse tools and accessories, you can plant almost anything anywhere.

GREENHOUSE

You can also take advantage of the autumn sun and plant salad crops and French beans.

Although the optimum temperature for most plants is between 75°F to 85°F (24°C to 29°C), vegetables like cabbage, broccoli, and peas can grow in temperatures below 40°F (4°C). Tomatoes and peppers grow well within 80°F to 85°F (27°C to 29°C) temperature range.

Getting Started

You can start small when planting your vegetables. If you haven't bought the containers and pots to plant seeds, you can improvise by getting clear plastic containers like the ones used for grapes or any other fresh fruits in a supermarket. The clear lid will act as a container for planting the seeds, which you can cover with a plastic wrap.

Based on the size of your greenhouse structure, you can plant multiple seeds on the benches or on the shelves. After planting, you can add and install lighting and other temperature control equipment in the greenhouse. You can use fluorescent lights to increase the amount of light in the greenhouse while boasting seedling growth.

Sometimes, it is good to disinfect the benches, shelves, pots, and trays before planting seeds on them. The moist environment inside can attract pests like fungi, algae, among others.

How to Grow Vegetables in the Greenhouse

Vegetables grown in your own garden will be the freshest. You can extend the growing season of spring and autumn by growing them in your greenhouse at any time. A greenhouse will allow you to control the temperature, humidity, water, and light, based on the needs of the vegetables. The type of vegetables to grow in your greenhouse will depend on your location and the temperatures within your greenhouse garden.

To succeed in cultivating vegetables, you must:

GREENHOUSE

1. Planning

Planning involves preparation of the seeding area in the greenhouse. You need to determine how much space you require for the growing beds and the grow bags' floor space. Ensure the greenhouse has enough space to separate spring plants from the summer vegetables you're planning to grow.

Prepare the benches to create more room for seedlings. You can move some crops outside during the summer to create more room for planting other vegetables.

2. Planting the Seeds

Plant the seeds in the pots or starting tray. Read all the instructions on the seed packet and follow the instructions to plant the seeds, then make sure to buy high-quality seeds from a trusted source. Seeds of high quality will increase the germination rate.

Put two to three seeds in a pot containing the seed-starting mix and avoid using regular soil, as it may contain some diseases or may not be good for the germination of the seeds. Water the pots by using a sprayer or a meat-basting syringe, and gently water the pot without causing soil disruption. After watering, cover the pot with a plastic material to prevent it from drying too quickly.

The seed-starting mix provides the best conditions for germination of the seeds. It is best for drainage and has an excellent water-holding capacity. It also minimizes diseases, which can affect any vulnerable seedlings.

The containers should have an adequate number of holes to facilitate draining and ensure the seeds are not waterlogged. You should keep the seed-starting mix moist at all times to allow the seeds receive enough air and water, which are essential for the seeds' growth.

Once you plant the seeds, place the pots or trays where there is direct sunlight. If the greenhouse has little sunlight, you can supplement it with artificial lights, such as a fluorescent light.

After the seedlings emerge, ensure the pots have good access to light and control the greenhouse temperatures according to the needs of the seedlings.

You can use a heated propagator to increase the warmth needed for the crop germination.

3. *Growing the Vegetables*

After the seedling show up, remove the plastic cover and put them where they can access light, as they will need a lot of light and a frost-free environment to continue growing. You need to ensure some sections of the greenhouse are properly heated to provide enough of a warm environment for the plants' growth, especially for tender vegetables.

Monitor the temperature of the greenhouse at all times.

GREENHOUSE

Some vegetables like broccoli grow within 50°F to 70°F (10°C to 21°C) during the day and between 45°F and 55°F (7°C and 13°C) at night. Warm-loving vegetables can tolerate day temperatures between 60°F and 85°F (16°C and 29°C) and 55°F to 65°F (13°C to 18°C) for night temperatures. Therefore, warm and cool vegetables may not survive in the same greenhouse temperatures, so you should always choose what to grow in each greenhouse and when.

You should also start the fertilization of the growing seedlings after every week. Organic fertilizers are highly recommended because they can provide a wide range of nutrients and micronutrients to the seedling.

If there are more seedlings in the pot, you can thin out the excess seedlings with scissors once the seedling has grown two sets of leaves. Always thin out the *weakest* one.

Each pot or container should have a single seedling for it to grow well, so continue to water the seedlings to allow them to grow.

4. Transplanting the Vegetable Seedlings

You need to plant the vegetable seedlings in their final location once they're well rooted in the soil. You can do this using large containers or growing bags to plant the crops. Offer extra care to the newly transplanted vegetables and ensure they're shaded from direct sunlight for a day or two or until they get established.

When transplanting the vegetable plants, make sure you place the pots with the tallest plants on the shelves at the back.

Ensure there is some space between each vegetable plant and water the vegetables regularly or when necessary. You should not leave the top soil dry for too long.

You must give vegetables like cucumbers and melons support as they climb up. You can tie one cucumber tree to another to give them more strength and to allow them to support one another. To support cordon tomatoes, tie them up with strings or canes.

5.   *Maintenance*

Make sure you water the vegetables well and daily, as uneven watering can affect some of the vegetables. For example, if certain sections of the tomato beds are not well-watered, it can result in rotting.

Ensure the greenhouse is well-ventilated and there is enough light inside to aid in the growth of the vegetables. You can install automatic vents or use the manual vents to keep the room well-ventilated.

You can open the door of the greenhouse or its windows to let fresh and cool air flow inside, which will help regulate the greenhouse's temperature. If there is too much heat lost in the greenhouse, you can reduce the heat loss by insulating all windows and doors.

If you have planted warm-loving vegetables such as cucumber or okra, make sure the vents remain closed and increase the humidity in the room. This makes certain that no moisture is retained, which can damage the vegetables. You can also partition some parts of the greenhouse with a clear, plastic material.

Make sure you keep the greenhouse clean at all times. Investing in bubble wrap insulation for your structure would be an excellent idea to address this concern.

If you're using a heated greenhouse, install a thermostat to maintain the greenhouse's temperature. This will ensure the minimum nighttime temperatures do not drop below the expected temperatures for the plants' growth. You should also install a two thermometers to monitor the minimum and maximum temperatures within the greenhouse. One thermometer will measure the temperature inside the greenhouse, whereas the second thermometer will measure the outdoor temperatures.

Always remember to tie up the vegetables to provide support for any new growth, especially if you are handling tomatoes in the greenhouse.

Be alert and watch out for pests, bugs, fungi, and any other diseases that can affect the plants in the greenhouse. If a fungal disease infects your garden, you should consult with professional services on the possible insect repellents to use.

Challenges You May Face

You may face soil problems like soil borne diseases, especially if you have been cultivating on the same type of soil for more than four years. Therefore, if you're growing vegetables in the greenhouse border, you can reduce the soil borne diseases by digging out the soil and replacing it with new soil or using a good garden loam.

You can try **grafted plants** if you have soil issues in your garden. In this case, tomatoes and aubergines will do well.

Another way you can reduce the soil borne diseases is by using pots and grow bags. You should cover the soil with a plastic sheeting, then place the pot or grow bag on top of it.

Some diseases that can affect the growth of your vegetables include: grey mould, powdery mildew, and damping off.

Some pests that may affect the vegetables include: glasshouse leafhoppers, red spider mites, and glasshouse whiteflies.

GREENHOUSE

What Vegetables to Plant and When

For your greenhouse to stay productive all year round, you need to take advantage of every plant growing season and diversify your garden.

Winter and Early Spring

If you have installed a heated greenhouse, you can plant **tomatoes** and **peppers** in one section of your garden. Use a heated propagator to aid in the germination of the vegetables.

You can plant frost tolerant vegetables like **cabbage**, **lettuce**, **onions**, **Brussels sprouts**, and **peas** as you wait for the warm weather. These vegetables can survive in low temperatures, and you can transplant them outdoors.

Mid-Spring Season

In mid-spring, you can prepare your garden to plant tender vegetables like **cucumbers**, **melons**, **pumpkins**, **courgettes**, and **sweetcorn**. Later, you would transplant the vegetables during the late spring or plant them outside in the early summer period.

These vegetables require a warm and more controlled environment for them to grow well, so install a heated propagator to ensure proper germination of the vegetables. If the plants are exposed to any front before you transplant them outdoors in the early summer, they will not survive the frost.

Early Summer Season

The summer season includes late spring and early summer season. During this season, you can transplant the mid-spring vegetables outdoors and create more space for planting midsummer vegetables.

When temperatures are favorable, you can plant **eggplants**, **hot peppers** and **tomatoes** in the garden. Although these are heat-loving plants, too much heat can affect some vegetables' growth and invite some molds in the greenhouse. It can also make some vegetables dry out.

You can transfer the vegetables outside once the frost is over.

In midsummer, you can harvest some of the vegetables grown like **cucumbers, melons,** and **French beans.**

Late Summer

During this season, you can plant more **potatoes** in the greenhouse. You can also grow **lettuce, carrots,** and **spicy salad leaves** to take advantage of the autumn sun and harvest some of the vegetables.

Autumn Season

Some activities done during this period include harvesting some of the vegetables grown in summer. You can grow **lettuce** in a grow bags and harvest them during the winter season. Other vegetables you can grow during this period include the **French beans, snow peas, kale,** and **calabrese.**

How to Determine the Best Soil for Planting Vegetables

Cultivating a strong soil foundation will enable you to harvest healthy and nutritious vegetables. Healthy soil with result in healthy vegetable and a healthy environment.

If you plant vegetables on a healthy soil, your cost for fertilization and pesticides will be less, and it will not only result in healthier vegetables, but it will also improve your own health.

A good organic soil is full of humus and is made from decomposed materials such as leaves, compost, and grass clippings. The decomposed materials increase nutrient and mineral values of the organic soil, making it ideal for growing plants.

Soil requirements for most vegetables are the same; although, there are certain types of vegetables that do better in certain types of soils. In this tutorial, I will discuss the general soil requirement for greenhouse garden. The best soil for cultivating vegetables is one that drains well and loose.

Determining Soil Health

Plants need nutrients like nitrogen, potassium, and phosphorus for their growth. We commonly term these nutrients as the **primary micronutrients** that plants absorb from the soil. Other nutrients like magnesium, calcium, and sulfur are referred to as the **secondary nutrients**. Although there are other nutrients present in a healthy soil, these are the most common nutrients and each performs a certain function in the growth of a plant.

Soil health can also be determined inform of its pH value; that is, you can have an acidic soil or an alkaline soil based on the pH reading. All the nutrients, soil texture, and soil pH contribute to making healthy soil.

Soil Testing

Soil testing is done to determine which minerals are present or lacking and the percentage of each mineral concentration. The tests measures soil pH, basic nutrients like calcium, potassium, magnesium, pHospHorus, nitrogen, and micronutrient content.

Most vegetables need a pH value of between 6 to 7. If the pH value is greater than 7, you need to lower the pH; if it's below 6, you have to raise the pH. The soil pH affects the growth of vegetables, and no matter how many nutrients the soil may have, the plants will not absorb the nutrients if the pH is outside of the recommended range.

You can test the soil pH to determine whether its

alkaline or acidic using pH test kits available in the market.

To get the accurate result on soil components and nutrients, it's best you test them during spring or fall season. This will enable you to know the soil components and whether to add any fertilizers to the soil or not.

You can balance the pH by:

Reducing soil acidity: If the test shows the soil has high acidity, you need to reduce excess acidity in the soil. One way of reducing acidity level is mixing the soil with limestone. Make sure to follow the manufacturer's instructions on the quantity you're supposed to use for every mix. You can add limestone each year at the beginning of every fall or during spring.

Increasing the pH level: When the soil is alkaline, you can add some additives like sulfur or gypsum to increase its pH. You can also apply compost material to the soil regularly to reduce its alkalinity. Make sure to always test the soil every time you add compost; otherwise, you may make the soil too acidic.

Soil Texture and Type

Apart from examining the soil pH, nutrients, and micronutrients, you need to determine its texture and type.

You would determine the by the amount of sand, silt, and clay present in the soil. Most soils have **sand** as its highest constituent, so when touched, it feels gritty. That is followed by **silt**, which is slippery when wet and looks powdery when dry. The component with the lowest constituent in is **clay**, with pieces that tend to stack together and look like sheets of paper.

You can buy a complete soil testing kit from any hardware store like Home Depot, or retail shops like Walmart. Make sure to follow the manufacturer's instructions to test the soil. Alternatively, you can determine whether the soil is sandy or silt with your hands. Pick some soil up from your garden and rub it together with your fingers—if the soil feels gritty, then it is probably sandy soil; if it feels smooth like powder, then it is silt. However, if it feels slippery or sticky when wet, or harsh when dry, then it is clay soil.

GREENHOUSE

Sandy soil is poor in nutrients and drains quicker due to its large particles. The soil also has a low number of micronutrients and organic matter, which are essential components for plants to thrive. Therefore, if you have this type of soil in your garden, consider improving its texture and nutrients before planting the vegetables.

Silty soil is more fertile and has all the nutrients and micronutrients required by the plants to grow, but it drains poorly.

Clay soil is dense, and plants may not grow well in this type of soil. There is no space between the clay particles affecting its drainage, and you will need to improve the soil to make it appropriate for plant growth.

Improving Soil

You can improve garden soil by adding organic matter. You can do this by adding compost and manure, or through mulching and growing cover crops. Adding organic matter to the soil will supply all the nutrients the plants need to grow, and it is the most recommended.

You can also add mulch and some green manure to make the soil healthier for vegetable growth. Adding fertilizers to the soil will only increase some nutrients in the soil and will not be ideal for maintaining it.

A good soil should have enough air held between its particles. Plants need air for their overall growth and photosynthesis. The amount of air in the soils has atmospheric nitrogen, which converts into a form used by the plants as they grow. Oxygen in the soil is also essential for the survival of certain soil organisms that contribute to the plants' growth.

Silt and clay soils has little air between the small particles, which are close together. You can increase the amount of air circulation between the particles by digging the soil to make it loose and mixing it with compost.

Sandy soil has big particles that allow a lot of air in. The only problem with sandy soil, however, is the rapid decomposition of the compost organic matter caused by excess air in the soil particles.

Adding organic matter to the soil helps balance the air supply in the soil, and most plants can grow well in soils with 25% of air. Organic matter can break the heavy particles of clay and silt soils and bind together the particles in sandy soil. This process helps improve the air supply in the soil and improve its retention of water and nutrients. Organic compost can also lower the pH level of the soil and create an environment perfect for growing vegetables.

Adding Fertilizers to the Soil

Organic fertilizers are the best compared to the synthetic fertilizers, but they take a long time before you can realize the benefits. They provide long-term supply of nutrients to the plants. Alternatively, you can use synthetic fertilizers, which only add nutrients to the soil for a short period of time. However, frequent use of synthetic fertilizers can have a negative impact on the soil in the long run, since liquid or dry fertilizers can kill all the microorganisms in the soil.

When adding fertilizers, follow the instructions on the label. You would mix dry fertilizer with the soil, according to the direction given, and once done with mixing them, you can water the soil. Different fertilizers have different a nutrient constituent, and each has the nutrients listed on the label.

If you're using liquid fertilizers, spray it directly to the plant or on the soil. Fish emulsion and seaweed blends are the most common liquid fertilizers in the market. Always read the instructions of every fertilizer before using it.

Watering Vegetables

Plants need water to survive, and vegetables are no exception. You should ensure you water the vegetable plants moderately to gain maximum yield.

Vegetables are best watered in the morning, which ensures full absorption of water by the vegetable roots. If you water during midday sun, there is a high chance of water evaporation before absorption. Watering at night encourages the growth of slugs and can introduce diseases such as blackspot and others.

You will need thorough watering to grow strong and healthy vegetables. Doing so ensures water penetrates deep into the soil, encouraging deep root development. A shallow watering at the surface will result in a weak and shallow root system.

Overwatering can create a perfect environment for growing diseases and encourage snails in the area, and excess water that runs off the soil can wash away soil nutrients, making the plants growing in that location have a weak and shallow root system.

If the soil doesn't drain well and you leave the vegetables in a waterlogged area for long, it will deprive them of oxygen, which is an essential component for their growth.

Always check the soil moisture to avoid overwatering the vegetables. If you grow the vegetables in containers or pots, ensure the containers have enough water drainage holes.

Seedlings require extra care. You need to keep the soil for planting the vegetables moist, and once you plant the seeds in the soil, carefully water them to avoid washing the seeds away. As the seeds grow, you can introduce drip irrigation to have a controlled watering. Another method is to dip the pot with the growing plant into a tray with water, which will allow the pot to soak water from below rather than watering from above. When the pot is fully soaked, you can remove it from the water tray and leave it to drain.

Sometimes, too much or too little water may make crops wither. If the soil above and below the surface is dry, you should water the crops immediately. If the crops are in an area where they experience direct sun, you can move the containers toward some shade or shade the entire area.

If the crops are withering due to excess water, check the drainage system. If the crops are on waterlogged soil, you can create more holes in the soil to aid in draining more water.

When planting, you should also group thirsty vegetables together to make your watering more efficient. Some thirsty vegetables include:

- Carrots
- Cucumbers
- Peas
- Beans
- Peppers
- Pumpkins

Pollination in Vegetables

Vegetables are self-pollinating plants and do not require insects or any animal pollinators to make their crops.

GREENHOUSE

A self-pollinating plant has both the **stamen** (from the male parts) and the **pistil** in the flower. A gentle breeze can transfer the male stamen to the female pistil, and once the pollinators come across these flowers, they facilitate the pollination process. In this type of pollination, you will find both the male and female flower parts on the same flower.

If there are no pollinators, you can complete the pollination process through hand pollination by either tapping on the vegetable stems or brushing your hands against the flowers as you walk by.

Some self-pollinating vegetables include:

- Eggplants

- Peppers
- Tomatoes
- Legumes, like beans and peas

Other plants that use cross pollination require the wind to move the male pollen (stamen) to the female pistil. They pollinate the flowers in the plant or use flowers from another plant.

Some wind pollinated plants include:

- Corn
- Wheat
- Oats
- Spinach
- Chard

Plants that grow from their roots and leaves require no pollination at all. This is because they do not depend on any flowers or seeds.

Some of these plants include:

- Potatoes
- Onions

- Carrots
- Broccoli
- Cauliflower
- Garlic
- Lettuce

All these vegetables grow only for their roots or the plant as a whole, like lettuce, and you should not pollinate them. If any of these vegetables grow flowers, you must remove them immediately.

Vegetables in the family of **cucurbit**, for example—cucumbers, pumpkins, muskmelon, and squash—require bee pollination because they have separate male and female flowers. Most of these vegetables have either the male flowers or the female flowers; therefore, they require pollinators to transfer the male pollen to the female stigma. If there are no pollinators, you can use a hand pollination.

With hand pollination, use a clean paintbrush to harvest pollen from the male flower, then transfer it to the stigma of the female flower. Always make sure to do hand pollination in the *morning*.

Animal pollinators can provide you with a long-term solution for pollinating cucurbit-type vegetables. Attract animal pollinators to your garden by creating a pollinator habitat within the yard or nearby to attract bees.

Examples of insect-pollinated vegetables include:

- Cabbage
- Kale
- Cucumbers
- Muskmelons
- Okra
- Celery

When using self-pollination on your vegetables, you produce **true-to-type vegetables**. That is, vegetables with the same size, color, flavor, and shape as the parent plant.

Cross-pollinated vegetables may produce a true-to-type vegetable, and sometimes, the crop may not grow to true after pollination.

Causes of Poor Pollination

Sometimes, the vegetables can have too many flowers but yield few fruits. This can be due to poor pollination, possibly caused by:

GREENHOUSE

- **Poor weather**: In cold areas, there are fewer insects to pollinate your plants; therefore, you must rely on hand pollination.

- **Frost**: If you're in an area that experiences frost, and you do not have enough heating equipment to regulate the temperatures, then the frost will affect the flowers and ruin the pollination process. You can solve this problem by spraying the flowers in the morning with ice cold water, which will slow down the rate of warming up the flowers and make them sprout out gently.

- **Access of insects**: Pollination may not take place because insects cannot access the greenhouse. You can keep the greenhouse open during sunny days to allow insects inside to pollinate the plants.

Chapter Summary

In this chapter, we went over various strategies for cultivating vegetables in the greenhouse. The chapter highlighted specific ways to:

- To plant vegetables using seeds in the greenhouse garden.

- Determine the best soil for planting vegetables, how to test the soil nutrients, how to determine the soil type and texture, and how to improve the soil.

- What to plant in the greenhouse and when.

- How to water vegetables.

- How pollination takes place in the greenhouse.

In the next chapter, you will learn how to cultivate herbs in the greenhouse.

CHAPTER SIX

CULTIVATING HERBS

Have you ever wanted to grow your own herbs in your backyard? With a greenhouse, growing herbs is completely possible, and there are various designs and styles you can choose from.

GREENHOUSE

Growing your own herbs ensures you have a constant supply of fresh herbs in your garden, which will serve you with medicinal and culinary benefits. They can help cure colds and boost your sleep, among curing diseases.

Herbs can also add taste and flavor to a variety of foods. You can use different herbs to produce different spices for adding taste to food.

You would not only add these herbs to your food, but you can also produce attractive flowers that make your garden look more beautiful.

Growing herbs is easy, as you only need to set up a greenhouse structure and you are good to go. Once you build a greenhouse to cultivate herbs, always remember cultivating herbs in the greenhouse is different from growing herbs outdoors because greenhouse plants require more attention than the outdoor plants.

Growing herbs in a greenhouse will allow you to:

Extend the herbs growing period: A greenhouse provides you with a controlled temperature environment that will allow you to plant herbs at any time, meaning that you will be able to grow and sell a lot of out-of-season herbs. Whether growing the herbs for personal use or sale, a greenhouse garden will ensure you have a constant supply.

Protect the herbs from pests: Having your own controlled greenhouse environment to plant herbs means don't have to worry about pests and other diseases affecting crops in the neighborhood. You can take measures to ensure you herbs stay safe from insects, rodents, and caterpillars.

Protect the herbs from harsh weather conditions: Greenhouses protect crops from extreme heat, strong winds, dust storms, and other harsh weather conditions. You can grow any crop in any unpredictable climate, provided you have all the equipment and tools needed to operate the greenhouse.

Prevent soil erosion: Another benefit of using a greenhouse is to protect your crops from any damage caused by flash floods, rainstorms, or any other condition that may affect the crops if left exposed.

Tips for Growing Herbs

Herbs can grow in any location, even in areas where there is freezing temperatures. All you need is a sheltered place or a greenhouse where you can control these extreme temperatures and extend the herbs' growing season.

To get healthy, all-year-round herbs you need to:

GREENHOUSE

1. **Water them regularly:** Always water herbs until the soil is moist, then leave them to dry out slightly before the next watering. From watering, they will develop a deep root system.

2. **Let them remain dormant for a while:** During the cold season, herbs are dormant; therefore, don't worry if you see the herbs perennial varieties turn brown at the top during that period. After a while, you can trim the brown parts and leave them to grow to their usual size during the spring season.

3. **Maintain fresh air in the greenhouse:** Ensure there is circulation of fresh air inside the greenhouse. You can open the door and greenhouse windows to let fresh air in or install vents. If you locate your greenhouse in a moist and wet environment, the stale air inside may encourage fungus and pests in the greenhouse. To avoid this potential outcome, keep the greenhouse well-ventilated and ensure there is a lot of fresh air inside.

4. **Pinch the herbs:** Pinching the flowing stem will keep the herb well-trimmed and bushy. It also prevents it from growing to seed and extends the herbs growing period. When flowers and seeds show up, it will automatically slow down the plants growth, and you will only be able to see a few leaves.

Basic Requirements for Herb Growth

Regardless of which herbs you want to grow in your greenhouse, there are various requirements for all herbs.

Setting up a greenhouse will enable you to grow all-year round herbs and control moisture, head, and shade for the herbs. However, the largest problem with herbs is lack of adequate moisture in the garden area. Therefore, you need to ensure there is adequate supply of moisture for the herb plants to succeed. To increase moisture, you must install a misting system and automatic drip hoses in the greenhouse. An automatic hose system makes sure that there is a frequent supply of water to facilitate the steady growth of herbs.

A system of shading the herb plants is another key component for the success of your herbs. If you already have an existing greenhouse, you can create a shading system by attaching rip-stop nylon or Velcro to the roof of the greenhouse. You can easily attach them with hooks and remove them when necessary.

When building a new greenhouse for growing herbs, don't roof it entirely with glass or plexiglass. You can roof some sections of the greenhouse with sunroof-type installations or use skylights, which are great for providing adequate air circulation in the greenhouse.

Set up artificial lights raised 2 to 4 inches away from the herbs. Herbs grow well in grow lights, which make the

GREENHOUSE

herb plants adapt easier to an outdoor climate.

Use the seed-starting mix to grow the herbs' seeds. The starting mix is lighter than the normal potting soil and makes the seeds germinate quicker. The starting mix increases the seeds' chances of survival and reduces the chance for infectious diseases, which can be caused by potting soil.

Plastic trays are the best for growing herb seeds, and the trays have small cells that make it easy to grow many herbs at a time. If you have herbs with the same growth requirements, you can grow them in the same area but in different sections.

You can transplant the herbs later into large clay pots. If you're planting herbs that do not require any transplant like Parsley, you can use a large clay pot when planting the seeds. Keep pots and seed trays in a warm area and away from direct sunlight.

Once you plant the seeds, cover them with a plastic wrap to keep the soil moist and speed up the germination process. After germination, remove the plastic cover and keep the trays in an area in which can access light.

If you want to keep the seedlings green and the roots strong, you can spray the herb plant with a light liquid organic fertilizer. You should do this one week after the germination of the seeds.

Growing herbs from their seeds is the most common

procedure. There is a wide range of seeds to choose from, with some suppliers selling organic seeds and others selling non-GMO seeds. Some herbs are also bee friendly.

Another option is to plant the herbs from their cuttings. You can cut a piece of an already-grown plant and plant it in a different place or share it with your neighbors.

How to Grow Herbs From Seeds

Growing herbs requires little maintenance once it is well-established. Each harvest produces an enough number of herbs you can use for a long time. Fresh herbs directly from the garden have a fresh fragrance and can add more flavor to your food.

You should grow herbs in a specific section in the greenhouse. Giving you more room to grow other vegetables.

You can cultivate herbs from seeds in your greenhouse, and growing herbs from their seeds is less expensive compared to buying herb seedlings. You will also have a wide variety of herbs to plant.

Planting the Seeds

1. You should soak the herbs' seeds in water for a whole day or leave them to soak in a container with water overnight.

2. Prepare the containers for planting the seeds and make sure the containers or pots have enough holes to drain water. Then, fill the container with the start mix soil.

3. Plant the seeds in the container with the start mix soil. You need to plant these seeds three times deeper than the normal seed planting depth. If the seeds are tiny, you can press them into the soil with your hands.

    Water the seeds, then cover the container with a plastic wrap. This will help retain moisture in the soil mix and speed up the seeds' growth.

You should take a lot of care when watering the planted seeds to avoid washing them away, and you can use a bottle springle sprayer to thoroughly water them while avoiding this outcome. Once you've watered them, you need not water them again until the seedlings appear.

Place the planted seeds in the container in an area with access to light.

4. Once the seeds grow, remove the plastic cover and water the seedlings. Ensure the containers are in a warm area and have access to sunlight.

5. If you have excess seedlings in a container, you can wait until two sets of leaves emerge, then remove the weak seedlings. If you want to transfer the seedlings to your garden, you can take the containers outside when the temperatures are warm to harden them. After a week, you can transfer the seedlings to your garden or outdoors.

6. You can also transplant the leaves by digging a hole where you want to transplant them and then pinching off the lower set of leaves on the plant.

The hole you make should be able to hold the plant up to where you had pinched the leaves.

You can then remove the plant from the container and transplant it in the hole. Turn the container upside down and carefully allow the plant to slide into your hands, while avoiding pulling the plant by its stem or leaves. Once you've removed it from the container, you can put it into the hole and add soil around the plant. The leaf nodes made from pinching the lower sets of the leaves will grow roots when transplanted.

Water the plant once daily for a whole week, and thereafter, water them twice on a weekly basis.

When the herb plant gets bushy, add mulch around it to avoid weed growth.

Soil Preparation

Although herbs can do well in almost any type of soil, having a good soil will help you maintain your garden easier. While many herbs will require little care, you will still need to prepare the soil for cultivating herbs in your garden.

A good soil for planting herbs should have 50% of solid material and 50% of porous space to provide enough room for holding air, water, and the herb plant's roots. The solid material comprises inorganic matter made of fine rock particles and organic matter made of decayed plants.

Inorganic soil particles are divided into three parts: Clay, silt, and sand.

Clay has the smallest soil particles among the three, followed by silt with medium-size rock particles, and sand with the largest number of soil particles. The amount of sand, silt, or clay in the soil determines the soil texture. For example, loam soil is a mixture of clay, silt, and sand in the ratio of 20:40:40%.

Soil Texture

To harvest better and healthier herbs, you need to improve the soil texture and structure. You can add organic matter to the soil to help the soil hold or drain more water.

You can use materials like sawdust, grass clippings, corncobs, straw, and cover crops as organic matter, and you can use your own compost as organic matter to enrich the soil nutrients.

Soil Testing

Similar to with vegetables and fruit, you also need to test the soil nutrients and pH level. You can collect soil samples from your garden and send them to a laboratory for testing, or use home soil testing kits that are available in the market. You can buy one and use it to test soil nutrients and pH level.

Home test kits come with an instruction manual for how to use them and how to read the results presented to determine your soil texture and nutrients. Some kits have information on how to get the soil samples for testing. Follow the instructions to test the soil in your garden.

Based on the test report, you can figure out the type of fertilizer to use for increasing soil nutrients in your garden. Test reports from a lab come with recommendations for the amount and type of fertilizer needed to improve the soil.

Soil test results will show the pH level of the soil, which is its acidic and alkaline balance. The pH level is measured on a scale of 1 to 14, with 1 representing more acidic and 14 as the most alkaline, whereas a scale of 7 shows neutral soil. Herbs grow best in a pH level of between 5.5 and 7.5. It will also show the percentage of nitrogen, potassium, and phosphorous in the soil.

The pH level determines the number of nutrients present in the soil. Soil labs test the type of soil, pH level, and the herbs you intend to plant and gives you a recommendation for the pH changes you need to make and the nutrients you should add to the soil to increase herb produce.

According to the pH report, you can adjust the pH level

by either raising or lowering it. You can raise the pH by adding lime to the soil at any time of the year, and you can lower the pH level by adding the recommended sulfur product to the soil.

Types of Herbs You Can Grow in a Greenhouse

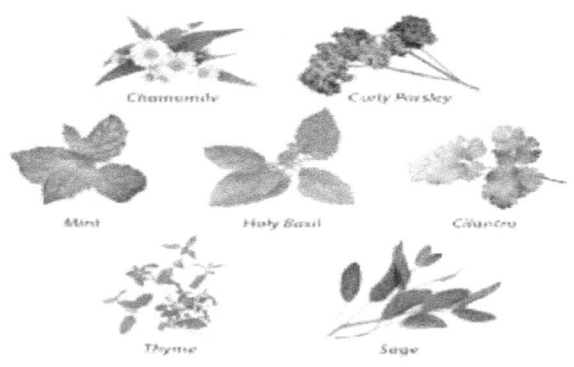

Tender annual herbs do well in an enclosed greenhouse structure. If you want to extend the growing season for other types of herbs, you can grow them in the greenhouse. Some of these herbs to grow include:

- Basil
- Dill

- Mints
- Lavender
- Parsley
- Chives
- Rosemary
- Thyme
- Cilantro
- Chamomile

Mints are an *invasive herb*; therefore, you must grow it in a container. There are various types of mints you can experiment with in your garden.

When planting herbs like rosemary, lavender, and bay, grow them in raised beds. Their roots may rot when left in moist areas, so ensure that you have good drainage system.

Fertilizing

Herbs grown outdoors require little fertilizer such as adding organic nutrients to boost the nutrients, whereas herbs grown in containers require fertilizers to produce a healthier plant and resist diseases and pests.

Herbs grown in containers use all the nutrients in the soil as they grow, and some nutrients may wash away as you water them. They also dry out quickly compared to those grown in a backyard. However, you can boost the nutrients by adding organic fertilizers to the soil at planting time. As the herb plant grows, you can use liquid fertilizer like fish emulsion to add more nutrients to the plant.

Organic fertilizers from plants and animals may take a lot of time before there is decomposition by microorganisms in the soil to provide nutrients to the plants, whereas inorganic fertilizers provide immediate nutrients to the plants.

Avoid over-fertilizing herbs. Too much fertilizer will result in herbs with bigger plants. It will also affect the essential oils important to adding flavor and aroma of the herb plant, thus diluting its flavor.

Watering Indoor Herbs

Water these herbs regularly. Monitor the herb garden daily, and if you notice the top of the soil dry, you should water the herbs immediately; do *not* overwater them. Overwatering can result to damping, which may make the bottom leaves of the herb to turn yellow.

You can employ an automatic watering system that gives the herbs a certain amount of water each day. This guarantees herbs' growth and makes them healthier.

Always water the roots of the herb and avoid pouring water to the leaves and its stalks because it can encourage fungal infection.

Herbs grown in containers need frequent watering, as the containers dry more quickly. Most herbs require watering three times per week or when an inch of the top soil feels dry. Pots placed outdoors may need daily watering due to the hot sun and wind, which makes the soil dry faster.

When using pots indoors, you can place them on drip trays to hold the water as it drains. Pour away the water from the trays after every irrigation process.

Pollination of Herbs

Some herbs, especially those used to add flavor to the food, do not need pollination. Only the leafy parts or the green part of the plant is needed to add to the food, not its seeds or fruits. However, seed-propagating herbs require pollination to take place to produce viable seeds.

GREENHOUSE

Herbs like thyme, rosemary, parsley, sage, and basil require pollination to produce seeds. Pollination can occur either through insect pollination or hand pollination.

How to Pollinate the Herbs

Stop pruning or pinching the herb leaves and let the herb plant develop flowers.

Once the flowers develop, they will attract insect pollinators like bees into your garden. 75% of herbs grown in a garden attract bee pollinators naturally; therefore, planting some of these herbs in the surrounding environment will attract bee pollinators to your garden. Just leave the greenhouse windows open and pollination will occur naturally.

Alternatively, you can take the herb plant outdoors and place it near other flowers where bees visit more frequently.

Strategies to Boost Pollination

If there is not enough adequate pollination, there will be little produce from the herbs. You can boost more pollination in your garden by attracting more pollinators, using wind pollination, or hand pollination.

1. *Plant Flowers to Attract Bees*

Bees are attracted to flowers, so planting different types of flowers in the surrounding area will attract different species of bees and other insect pollinators. Avoid cultivating double flowered plants because they make it difficult for the bees to access the flowers. These plants acts as the natural habitat for the bees, and once drawn into your garden, they will pollinate the herb plants.

Some of the herbs that attract bee pollinators include: basil, sage, lavender, germander, thyme, rosemary, lemon balm, and chamomile.

In an area with good sun and less wind, butterflies can pollinate the herbs. Some herbs that attract butterflies in the garden include: chives, mint, parsley, catmint, and thyme.

2. *Wind Pollination*

Some herbs rely on wind to carry the male pollen to the female flower. The pollen falls on the female parts, then the pollination takes place. You can facilitate wind movement in the greenhouse by shaking or tapping the plant from its stem.

3. *Hands Pollination*

Although hand pollination is rarely needed with herbs, you can still use it. During the cold or wet seasons when bees are unavailable, you can use a paintbrush to gather the male pollen and transfer it to the female stigma of the herb flower. You should do this practice early in the morning before the pollen dries up or extreme heat can affect it.

You can also remove the flower and strip off the flower

petals, then rub it against a female flower. Make sure you're rubbing on the female flower, as some plants have separate male and female flowers. The female flower has a swelling behind it.

Herbs grown out from cutting, like rosemary and perennial, propagate easier.

Watering Herbs

Just like your vegetables and fruits, herbs require moderate watering. Some herbs only need a single, deep watering per week, while others need regular watering.

Overwatering the herbs will kill them because they cannot handle excess water, and it is one of the principal mistakes many herb gardeners make.

How to Know the Herbs Have Been Overwatered

Herbs thrive well in semi-dry soil, which makes them able to withstand extreme drought in Mediterranean areas or dry climates.

Pay close attention to the herbs—if the herb plants start to wilt but the soil looks wet, you are probably overwatering the herbs. Other signs that can show you're overwatering include:

- The herb leaves turning yellow and starting to fall.

- The leaves turning black or dark in color.

- The herb plant has a fuzzy, mildew substance, like it has been infected with a mildew pathogen.

- The herb roots and stems starting soften and break. Rotted roots due to excess water become a gray or brown color.

- No growth shown, and there is no change to the herb after many days.

- Edema signs appearing, like blisters or lesions, on the herbs' leaves.

If the plant shows any of these signs, check on the drainage system first. If there is any standing water, you need to drain it immediately to avoid rooting of the herb roots and prevent breeding of pests, bacteria, and fungi in the area.

How to Avoid Overwatering

Different herbs require different water needs; therefore, it is essential to group the herbs based on these water needs. There are herbs that require a high amount of water, whereas others need less water. Know which type of herb you want to plant and identify its water needs, as knowing this will enable you to water more herbs more efficiently.

The rule is to water deep once in a while but less frequently. This ensures you grow deep rooted herbs that can withstand any weather condition.

Ensure there is proper drainage even in the potted herbs. If the soil drains poorly, improve the soil drainage by adding organic matter. You should do this before planting the herbs.

Always dip a finger an inch or two into the potting medium; if it's dry, water the herb plant at the root base. This reduces evaporation of water and prevents diseases caused by moisture in the pot media.

Herbs like basil and parsley can help you determine the watering schedule, as they can tell you when they need water by dropping the leaves. Once watered, they spring back to life in minutes. If you neglect them for too long, the leaves turn yellow and there is nothing you can do to recover the herb.

GREENHOUSE

Chapter Summary

Cultivating herbs indoors is simple and enables you to have access to the herbs' medicinal value at your fingertips. Herbs can also add flavor and taste to your food. Whatever location you are in, you can grow any type of herb in your garden or indoors. You can grow herbs from either seeds or seedlings.

Different herbs do well in different types of soil, and determining the best soil for the herbs is essential for increasing their produce. It also helps you figure out the type of herbs to grow and when.

There are insect-attracting herbs you can grow in your garden for which you won't have to worry about pollination.

A wide range of herbs can survive in almost any type of soil and require less fertilization. When grown indoors, the herbs are less infected by insects and pests. You should also water the herbs regularly.

Herbs require extra care when watering. Always make sure you're not overwatering them and that you have good drainage system in place.

In the next chapter, you will learn how to maintain the greenhouse.

CHAPTER SEVEN

MAINTAINING YOUR GREENHOUSE

Installing the greenhouse and planting crops on it is not all you must do—you must also keep the greenhouse in tip-top shape! You would do this with regular cleaning and maintenance of the greenhouse.

GREENHOUSE

Once every year, carry out a thorough cleaning of the greenhouse, as a high amount of moisture and dampness can lead to the growth of fungus, molds, algae, or mildew on the greenhouse walls. If left unchecked for a long time, they can spread throughout the entire greenhouse and infect the crops.

These molds and fungi not only infect the crops, but they can also cause health problems to individuals. Therefore, periodic maintenance of the greenhouses is crucial for the growth of healthy crops and maintaining one's own health too.

How to Maintain the Greenhouse

Remove Bugs and Pests

Wash all the benches in the garden with soapy water. Washing the benches and any other table in the greenhouse will enable you to remove dirt and moisture that can cause mold.

Always ensure you keep the surface of the greenhouse dry, and you can use cloth or a sponge to wipe clean any moisture or damp areas on the surface. Spray any built up mildew on the walls with the mildew spray. You should also clean the area between the panes to avoid buildup of condensation, which can lead to a growth of molds and algae.

Clean the flooring area of your structure thoroughly. Some floors are made of wood, gravel, cement, or fabric carpeting, and depending on your greenhouse's floor type, molds can grow. You need to scrub the floor and clean out any mold, mud, and other decaying matter.

Remove any dead plant branches and leaves. Pests or bugs can infect plants, causing the leaves to wither, and prune any dead leaves or branches to prevent further spread of the disease. You must take the dead leaves out of the greenhouse as soon as possible because if left inside, they may decompose and allow pests or bugs into the greenhouse.

Weeds and any other unimportant plants around the greenhouse area should be removed.

If some pests invade your greenhouse, you can release spiders and ladybugs into the garden, if they are available in your area. If ladybugs are not available in your pet stores, you can use pesticide to deal with pests in the greenhouse instead.

Provide Shade and More Sun

Most greenhouse roofs and windows are made of plastic

material or fiberglass. After some time, these materials can turn a darker shade caused by overheating from sun or microscopic molds. This change can reduce the amount of light into the greenhouse.

You should periodically clean the windows to allow more light and sun enter the greenhouse. Consider replacing the roof material after a while.

Plant trees that can provide shade for your greenhouse during the summer months, which can act as shade to protect your plants from hot weather. You should plant the trees on the west side of the greenhouse to block the sun and excess light into the structure. During the winter, the trees shed off the leaves, which allows extra sun to get into the greenhouse.

Alternatively, you can install roll-up shades. Roll-up shades are closed during the summer to protect the plants from the sun and remain opened in winter to allow more sun and light enter.

GREENHOUSE

Heating and Ventilation Problems

Greenhouses provide a temperature-controlled environment to meet the needs of your plants. You need to maintain the heating and ventilation equipment and ensure they're working properly. Check the equipment regularly and do full maintenance on them before the winter growing season.

If there are any gaps in the greenhouse exterior, you can use new glass panes to fill out the large holes or caulk to fill small holes in the exterior. This ensures heat you maintain heat inside the greenhouse.

Paint all walls black, as doing so makes sure that you attract and retain more heat.

GREENHOUSE

You can install roof vents between the ceiling and the rooftop. In most greenhouses, hot air is always trapped at the top part of the ceiling and prevent the crops from receiving enough warmth. Installing vents can easily push away hot air and allow fresh air from the outside in, thus increasing fresh air circulation inside.

You can also use fans installed diagonally at the opposite corners of the greenhouse, which increase fresh air circulation inside. Switch off the fans in the winter to conserve heat.

You should also consider a watering system or piping system. Make sure you properly install the water system and that it works as desired. You must also do frequent maintenance on the pipes to ensure no leaks.

Weed Control

Weeds growing in the greenhouses and other covered structures is one of the most persistent problems that many farmers face. These weeds affect the quality of plants grown, and other types of weeds can act as hosts for pests like whiteflies, snails, mites, and slugs.

Weeds that grow under the benches inside the greenhouse will usually host some pests and fungi; therefore, you need to come up with mechanisms to control the weed growth.

Removing the weed from the greenhouse benches, pots, and even the floor is important in the management of the greenhouse and maintenance of its aesthetic. A ground cloth put under the benches is highly recommended for weed management.

An accumulation of potting media on the ground can appear that will act as the perfect environment for weed growth if you do not collect it. A ground cloth can make it easy to collect the spilled potting media and prevent any germination of weed seeds.

Weeds that have already grown under the benches may force you to have to use herbicide to help manage them. There is a wide variety of herbicides in the market, but the majority of them are for outdoor use, while very few are for indoor use. Don't be tempted to buy the ones labelled for use outdoors, as it may have negative effects to the crops grown inside. In extreme cases, it can affect you plants in the next season. Vapor from some of the traditional herbicides can be trapped inside the structure and will not only affect the crops, but they could also be a health hazard to the people working in the greenhouse.

When applying greenhouse herbicides on the benches, read the instructions carefully. There are two types of herbicides in the greenhouse: **Pre-emergence activity** and **Marengo**. You can apply the herbicide labelled "pre-emergency activity" when the crop is present, and you can water the plant pot even after application. You should not apply BareSpot herbicides on the pot.

You cannot use Marengo herbicide when the plant is present; instead, apply Marengo herbicide before the start of the next growing season. Watering the area with the applied herbicide activates its residual compound, which can damage plants in the area due to volatilization from the herbicide.

Prevention Measures

You should come up with weed management program that allows you to regularly monitor the potting, plant holding, propagation, and the surrounding areas for the presence of weeds.

Before removing the weeds, identify the weed type, its

life cycle, and the area where its growing. Always make sure to manually remove weeds from the pots and benches after the plants flower and produce seeds.

The best weed control measure is through weed **sanitation**; that is, keeping away any weed propagules (like seeds, and rhizomes) in the greenhouse structure by using sterile media and cleaning plant materials. You should also control weeds growing outside the greenhouse.

Building concrete floors or having mulched floors will limit weed growth on the floors.

You can manually pull the weeds and prevent them from reaching the seed area in the greenhouse too. Mow the outside to control the weeds outdoors.

Use weed block fabric, which will act as a physical barrier to prevent weed establishment on the floor or under the benches.

You should also use weed-free potting soil. If the container or planting pots spill the potting media, clean them.

In areas where weeds continue to be a problem, you can remove the soil in that area or cover the area with mulch to prevent growth of the weeds.

Weed Management

Managing the weed growing conditions is essential for every greenhouse. A weed-free environment reduces the need for pesticides and increases production of high quality crops. Proper weed control practices help keep pests, insects, and weed diseases at bay.

Weeds compete with your crops for light, water, and nutrients; therefore, you should remove them as soon as possible before they affect your crops' growth. These weeds carry their own viruses too, which can damage or infect your crops.

A weed management program will help you to manage and control the weeds in your greenhouse effectively while helping you come up with control measures.

Sources of Weed Seeds

Weeds come from a variety of sources, some of which include:

- Ventilation fans blowing weed seeds from outside into the greenhouse.

- Contaminated seeds.

- Infected plants transplanted in the greenhouse from an external source.

- Poor plant growing area and storage or using dirty pots and containers.

- Contaminated or uncovered soil from under tables and benches.

- From the irrigation systems and water ponds.

How to Prepare Your Greenhouse for the Winter Season

Winter comes with slow activities after a productive summer. After the spring rush and the summer harvest, the actions you take on your greenhouse will determine how easy your next year's spring period rolls around.

If you want to reduce the amount of work during the next spring frenzy, you have to start preparing your garden for the winter.

To prepare for the winter, there are various things you need to check:

1.   *Move Out harvested Plants and Tools*

Fruits and vegetables that you have already harvested need move out of the greenhouse to create more room for the subsequent season plants.

You should take any pots, containers, seed trays, or any other tools that you are not currently using out for cleaning. Give them a proper scrubbing to remove all the dirt before taking them back to the greenhouse.

Once you have moved out everything out from the greenhouse, clean the structure itself. If you have been planting directly in the greenhouse soil, remove it and replace it with fresh soil and new compost. Doing this helps eliminate any unwanted weed seeds, pests, insects, and diseases established in the soil.

2. *Removing Rotten Plants and Weeds*

Remove all rotting plants in the greenhouse. Pests and insects feed on the crops during the summer period, and they may lay eggs on the plants or on its leaves; therefore, removing these plants and leaves from the soil will help you get rid of pests.

If the fallen plant leaves are disease-free, you can deposit them in the garden trench and convert them to organic matter.

Remove all established weeds from your structure. You can dig them up and burn them outside. Some invasive weeds remain in the compost matter, so avoid moving the compost from one area of the garden to another.

3. *Cleaning the Inside Out*

Thorough cleaning of the greenhouse is crucial. If there are still plants in the greenhouse, move them to a warm area and scrub all corners of the structure. You can use hot water and Jeyes fluid disinfectant, which is greenhouse-friendly. Make a plastic dirt-clicking tool to enable you flick dirt from the frames.

You should clean both the inside and outside of the greenhouse, as it not only makes your greenhouse sparkle cleans, but it also allows more light and warmth to enter the greenhouse.

After cleaning, leave the door and windows open to allow fresh air in and so the greenhouse can dry out fast.

4. *Moving Tools Inside*

Once the inside of the greenhouse is dry, you can return all the greenhouse tools you took out for cleaning (pots, trays, and containers). Then, you can decide what to do with the greenhouse.

You can move frost-sensitive plants inside to give them more warmth during the winter months, especially if you have a heated greenhouse. If you don't have a heated greenhouse, you can provide more warmth to the plants by using bubble wrap.

5. *Prepare the Soil for the Spring*

Fall is the best time to prepare your soil while you wait for the spring season. You can do this through adding compost, manure, and rock phosphate, among other substances to the soil to boost its nutrients and texture.

You don't have to wait until spring to enrich the soil with the required nutrients. It also helps in improving the drainage system before the busy season.

After preparing the soil and making all the adjustments, you can cover the area with a plastic sheet to prevent heavy winter rains from washing away the soil amendments.

6. *Planting Cover Crops*

During this period, you can sow cover crops, which helps prevent soil erosion in the area and increase organic matter in the soil bed. Planting cover crops increases nutrients in the soil, so for example, planting legumes or field peas will add to the level of nitrogen in the soil.

7. *Trim Perennial Plants*

The fall season is the best for pruning perennial plants in the garden. Although this depends on the kind of plant, raspberry plants continue to grow into the winter, whereas you are better off trimming blueberry plants during spring. You can trim herbs like rosemary and thyme during the fall. Blackberries can also benefit from the winter cleaning.

8. *Regenerate Compost*

After the summer harvest, you can use the compost material from the harvested plant trees and leaves to enrich the garden bed. This increases soil nutrients and can solve soil deficiencies. This practice will make your work easier as you jumpstart to the busy spring period.

Cleaning used compost in the garden makes way for new compost with more active microorganisms and green matter.

9. Adding Mulch to the Soil

Mulching helps prevent water loss by improving soil drainage, preventing soil erosion, and preventing the growth of weeds in your garden. Winter mulching helps regulate soil temperature and retain moisture. As the weather changes, the soil transitions to match the cold weather. The earth freezing can affect the plant roots; therefore, adding mulch to the soil will help regulate the temperature and save the plants' roots from freezing the Earth's surface.

If you have vegetables left in the garden during the fall season, you can add a layer of mulch to the vegetable root soil and prolong the crops' growth.

10. Review the Growing Season

This practice requires you to review the performance of the fruits and vegetables planted during the season. You would evaluate which fruit trees did better based on the produce, and which fruit did well. From this information, you can discern the kinds of fruits and vegetables to grow in your next season.

GREENHOUSE

You will also know which crops to add to the greenhouse to extend your harvest. You can choose to add crops that ripen early or late.

When comparing the performance to choose the next type of vegetables to plant, take notes on what worked for you and what didn't work and check what caused failure or success for each plant.

11. *Maintenance of Tools*

You may find it difficult to do maintenance on equipment during the busy seasons. During the fall, however, you can clean and remove debris from all your garden equipment. Remove rust with sandpaper, oil them, and sharpen the shovels with a mill file. Oiling the tools helps extend the tools' lifespans.

Chapter Summary

In this chapter, we learned about the different ways to clean the greenhouse and how to maintain the correct temperatures for your fruits and vegetables' success. We went over the various of managing and maintaining a greenhouse.

The chapter highlighted weed management techniques, how weeds can encourage pests and insects, the sources of weeds, how to control weeds established in the greenhouse, along with prevention measures.

From the chapter, you now know various strategies for managing your greenhouse garden during the winter season and how to prepare the garden for the next spring.

In the next chapter, you will learn more about pests and diseases control.

CHAPTER EIGHT

PESTS AND DISEASE CONTROL

One of the major problems many greenhouse farmers face is controlling pests and diseases in their gardens. Pests and diseases can affect plant production, so knowing how to manage these pests and control the spread of diseases can help for a more profitable farm.

Pest Management

Pests are any unwanted organisms in the greenhouse. Pests can affect the normal functioning of plants, and they include weeds, algae, spider mites, insects, and any other organism that can damage plants in the greenhouse.

Many farmers come up with an integrated pest management program to help them solve the problems they have in their farms. Coming up with an integrated disease management system will enable you to identify a wide range of measures you can use to control and prevent all types of diseases.

For any prevention measures to take place, you need to identify the potential infection to the crops. Doing this step will minimize the risk of infection and reduce the spread of the disease to other crops.

Integrated pest management involves coming up with a set of practices to manage and control pests. Controlling pests in the farm will enable you to have healthy and productive crops. Pests and diseases can affect the normal functioning and development of the crop, so controlling these pests and diseases will make the crop more productive.

Conditions Necessary for Disease Occurrence

- Presence of a pathogen.
- Favorable environmental conditions for the pathogen to survive.
- Plant susceptibility to the disease.

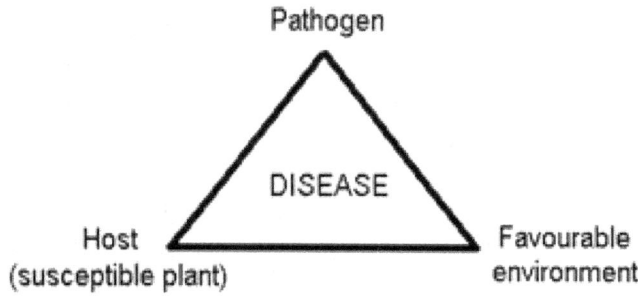

In the disease and pest control triangle, if you can control one or more of these conditions, you are a step closer to controlling the pest (pathogen).

You can control pests in the farm either through the use of pesticides or maintaining good hygiene in the farm. Changing the environmental conditions so they are unfavorable to the pathogen will limit its growth. You can also plant pest resistant crops in the farm.

Maintaining Greenhouse Hygiene

Maintaining the hygiene of the greenhouse is one of the most effective methods you can use to keep pathogens at bay. All the containers, pots, materials, and any other equipment brought inside the greenhouse should be clean.

Installing a foot bath is also essential, especially when

dealing with a commercial greenhouse. You should maintain the foot bath and change the disinfectant solution often, as this will minimize the risk of pathogens into the greenhouse.

Alternatively, you can empty the greenhouse and thoroughly clean it as you prepare for the fall season or between crops. Full cleaning of the structure helps remove any pathogens and diseases in the soil compost.

Use Disease-Free Plants

One source of pests is through contaminated seeds. Always buy seeds from trusted sources to avoid bringing pests to your farm through this medium.

When buying seedlings for transplant in your garden, inspect them upon delivery. If you are satisfied and they are disease-free, you can take them inside your greenhouse. Always make sure the storage area is clean and store the seedlings as they await transplant.

If any of the delivered seedlings looks infected, put it in a sealed plastic bag and take it for further testing. Do not plant any infected or potentially infected plants to avoid a spread of pests and diseases to the rest in your greenhouse.

You should also plant pest resistant crops. Most crops are tolerant to downy mildew and powdery mildew diseases.

Control the Growing Environment

Making the conditions unfavorable for the pest to survive in the greenhouse environment is the most effective method of pest control. Controlling the temperature and humidity limits the replication of diseases in the greenhouse.

Monitor the plants regularly to identify any early infection of the plants. This will enable you to take control measures before the pathogens completely damage the plant or spread across the entire greenhouse.

You should throw away pruned material or any other crop residual. Don't leave them to pile in the greenhouse—put all pruned material into disposal bags and throw them out, away from the greenhouse to avoid creating a breeding environment for pathogens. Immediately bury any crop debris from the greenhouse.

Remove weeds growing inside and outside the greenhouse, as weeds can provide a breeding place for pests, insects, and diseases. Removing weeds will help control insects that carry diseases into your plants.

Control Entry to the Greenhouse

You will find most greenhouse pests near doorways, as people can carry these pests and pathogens with them on their clothes and shoes while they walk around. Limit access to the greenhouse, so only a few people can enter.

If there are people visiting your greenhouse, give them disposable overalls to wear and let them pass through the installed foot bath. Avoid inviting visitors coming directly from other farms into your own farm because they may carry a lot of pathogens from their farm and bring them to yours.

Visitors should move from the young and healthy plants in the greenhouse to the older plants. This reduces the risk of spreading pathogens through the greenhouse.

Tips for Pest and Disease Control

1. Determine the Vulnerability of the Plants

Monitor your crops to know when they are vulnerable to pathogens. For example, bacterial diseases affect crops when their leaves sprout out, but they are less likely to affect the plant after the latter's maturity or propagation stage. Crops are also vulnerable to diseases when in the storage room awaiting to be shipped.

2. Determine Which Biocontrol Agents are Suitable for Your Farm

GREENHOUSE

You should know the best biocontrol agent to use for all your gardening operations. Different biocontrol agents affect pests in different ways; therefore, choosing the best biological control will help you control the pests in your garden.

3. *Sanitation of the Greenhouse*

You should prioritize your greenhouse's sanitation as a defense mechanism against all pests and pathogens. Sanitation involves cleaning the structure to avoid the spread of diseases, removing all plant debris, and weeding the inside and outside of the structure.

4. *Choose the Right Insecticide.*

There are different types of insecticides used for pest management. Before choosing which type of insecticide to use, determine the common pest problems you face in the greenhouse, when you harvest, and your ultimate plant produce goal. This will help you choose the correct insecticide for your needs.

5. *Establish Consistency in Pest Control*

Be consistent in pest control measures, as this will lead to a reduced cost for maintaining the greenhouse. It also ensures you can keep an ideal temperature and humidity within the structure.

Integrated Pest Management Techniques

Integrated pest management includes a systematic approach to solving pest issues in the farm. It provides long-term prevention mechanisms and control measures for handling pests and other pathogens in the farm.

These approaches include:

- Monitoring pest infestation.
- Identifying the types of pests in the farm.
- Coming up with control measures.
    - Biological control
    - Chemical control
    - Sanitation
    - Mechanical control measures
- Follow up/evaluation.

Monitoring Pest Infestation

This step involves assessing the pest infestation in the farm. It also determines potential pest infestations on your plants. Always do a thorough assessment each day to determine the status of the crops based on its appearance. Keep note of the appearance of the plant and any slight change, and you should also know the signs or symptoms of various potential pests. Daily monitoring of the plants is the key to coming up with early prevention measures.

Identify the Type of Pests Affecting the Crops

When pests infest crops they damage the normal functioning of the crop. Similar to weeds, pests inside the greenhouse compete with the plants for water, light, and nutrients. Different pests affect plants differently; therefore, the plant damage or injury will depend on the type of pest infested in the plant. These pests can include:

1.   Insects and Spiders

Insects eat on the plant leaves and other parts of the plant. They also nest on the plants' parts and are often invisible. It's important to know how each pest affects the plant to know which signs to look for in determining the type of pest you are dealing with.

2.   Diseases

Some common diseases affecting plants in the greenhouse include: fungi, viruses, and bacteria.

3.   Environmental Conditions

Some environmental conditions are favorable to the

growth and spread of pathogens within the greenhouse, and different environmental conditions encourage different pest infestations in the greenhouse. Some conditions include:

- Little or too much water.
- Little or too much light.
- Nutrient deficiency in the soil and phytotoxicities.

4. Weeds

The presence of weeds in the greenhouse will cause deficiencies in the crops sown. It competes for nutrients with the crops, limiting the amount of nutrients a plant needs to grow.

Weeds also provide a conducive environment for breeding pests. Always come up with consistent weed control and prevention mechanisms in the greenhouse. Weeds such as prostrate spurge and woodsorrel affect plant produce.

5. Algae

This is a dangerous that affects the people working in the greenhouse; however, it doesn't have any effect on the crops.

6. Snails and Slugs

Snails and slugs affect the younger crops in the greenhouse, and they eat the soft parts of the plants.

7. *Nematodes*

Nematodes affect the roots of the plant, as they make the roots of the crop swell and knot.

Control Measures

After monitoring the crops and identifying pests affecting them, the next step is to come up with control measures to solve these issues. You can take action that is: biological, chemical, mechanical, or with sanitation processes.

Biocontrol Measures/Biological Controls

Biocontrol measures rely on the use of biological agents to control the growth of pests in the greenhouse. These agents are safer than chemical agents and they include plants, animals, and microbes.

They have some beneficial organisms such as predatory insects and microorganisms, and fungi, and you can use any of these predators to control pests in the greenhouse. Biocontrol has less of an impact on the environment.

Chemical Control Measures

This method uses products with chemicals such as pesticides and insecticides to control pests. There are two types of pesticides: those labelled for general use and those labelled for restricted use.

You can buy the general use pesticide at any garden retail center, and they will be safe to use within your greenhouse. Restricted use pesticides are restricted to use under the supervision of a certified applicator. Its uses are also restricted.

Mechanical Control Measures

Mechanical control processes use hands-on and exclusion methods to control pests; that is, handpicking and destroying the pests in the greenhouse.

Exclusion processes involve closing the doors to ensure pests don't enter inside the greenhouse.

Cultural/Sanitation Processes

Sanitation methods of pest control ensure the environmental conditions are unfavorable for breeding of pests. Having a well-organized, clean, and sanitized environment is an effective way of managing pests. Ensure there is proper temperature control measures, a watering system, and a good fertilization of plants.

Follow-Up/Evaluation

In this step, you take a record of all the methods used in assessing, identifying the pests, and the actions taken. This information is valuable and you can use it to make future decisions in terms of pest management.

Rules for Pesticide Application

When using pesticides, always follow the instructions on the product label. Pesticides are harmful to humans and the environment; therefore, failure to follow those instructions and directions can be hazardous.

You should also warn the workers or people who have access to the greenhouse prior to the application. The warning can be oral or written, and you would use it a protective mechanism for those accessing the greenhouse.

Giving an oral followed by a written warning in highly recommended. You should notify employees about when the pesticide application will take place, instructions not to enter the treated area, and for how many days.

You can put warning signs in areas where everyone can see. If you applied the pesticide in certain sections, there should be a clear description of the treated area or section, and the information for when employees can resume access to those areas.

When applying pesticides, ventilation is crucial. Open the vents while you are spraying the plants, so the fresh air concentration inside is equivalent to the inhalation exposure level as stated on the product label.

Managing Diseases

Managing greenhouse diseases requires proper diagnosis of the diseases and pathogens that have infected your plants, where they came from, and the pathogen biology process. This information will guide you in choosing the right fungicide or pesticide to control the pathogen.

Fungicides manage the spread of diseases in the greenhouse. There are two types: those that act as protectants and those that work as eradicants or are curative.

Protectant fungicides work on the surface of the plant and gets into contact with the pathogen to destroy or control it. Plants require a regular protectant spray application for protection and growth. This type of fungicide can control a wide range of fungal diseases.

On the other hand, plants absorb **eradicant fungicide**. The chemicals control pathogens some distance away from where it landed on the plant. Unlike protectants, you should not apply eradicant as often, as continued use of these pesticides can lead to resistance in the fungal population.

Be careful when spraying pests in the greenhouse because bacteria and some fungi can spread by a moving spray mist, which forms after applying the pesticide. If some pathogens are resistant, then spraying them will only complicate the situation.

Common Sources of Diseases

The common pathogen sources include:

- Infested soil or potting mixture.
- Pathogens from the previously infected crops.
- All-year plants.
- Infected water.
- Pathogen spread through the air.

Infested Soil

Many pathogens and plant diseases in the soil. When you use infested soil in the potting mixture, nutrients in the plants will activate these pathogens; therefore, you should always make sure the potting mix is free from any pathogens before planting your crops. Treat the mixture to kill all the diseases before planting crops on it and ensure you keep all the potting media, benches, shelves, and other tools clean.

Soil from the surface or under benches may also be contaminated, and you should take care to ensure this soil doesn't come into contact with the potting mix.

Debris From Previously Infected Crops

Sometimes, when the conditions are not favorable for survival of pathogens such as extreme temperature or lack of adequate moisture, the pathogens can stay dormant in dead plant leaves, the stem, or on the roots. The dead plant tissues protect the pathogens from the harsh conditions and surface once more when the conditions are favorable.

Some fungi and bacteria can survive for several months in the plant debris. Leaving the infested debris inside the greenhouse may cause the disease to recur.

GREENHOUSE

All-Year Plants

All-year plants in the greenhouse can act as the hosts for pathogens. Viruses and other pathogens depend on living plants to grow and reproduce; therefore, keeping all-year plants in the greenhouse can be a reservoir for these viruses to sprout out from whenever the conditions are favorable for their growth.

Water

Water is the leading cause of pathogens such as pythium. These pathogens make the roots and stem of the plant rot. Water from the lakes, rivers, and ponds may be contaminated with various fungi and bacteria, and once you use them for irrigation, they can bring these pathogens into the greenhouse.

Air

In some cases, pathogens are brought into the greenhouse by air currents from outside plants. Infected plants and weeds near your greenhouse can be the source of pathogens, and it is difficult to prevent floating organisms carried by water. However, you can create an unfavorable environment within the greenhouse to prevent the survival of the disease-causing pathogens.

Make sure to clear the grass and weeds near your greenhouse. Use herbicides outside the greenhouse with caution, as their vapors can be drawn into the greenhouse by fans and air currents and can affect your plants.

Disease Preventive Measures

To control diseases in the greenhouse, you need proper sanitation and a keen eye. Pay a lot of attention to the growth of the crops and note down any slight change. You may have health problems and sudden bacteria growing inside from air infecting the plants. Without preventing measures and preparation, even the tiniest disease can cause huge damage to the crops.

It is not easy to get rid of fungus and bacteria that are affecting your crops quickly, but you can minimize the risk the bacteria will have in your greenhouse.

You can minimize the risk through:

- Proper sanitization of containers, potting media, shelves, stands, and any other tools you use inside the greenhouse.

- Clean the greenhouse surfaces regularly. This can help prevent spore germination in the structure.

GREENHOUSE

- Monitor the temperatures and humidity inside and ensure the greenhouse environment is not prone to disease.

- Ensure there is proper ventilation by increasing the supply of fresh air circulation inside.

- Make sure there is enough space between the plants to increase air circulation around them.

- Avoid water splashing on your plants; only water them at the base or on their crowns.

- Monitor new seedlings to ensure they are disease-free.

- Check the crops daily for any signs of disease, discolorations, or any other symptoms.

Common Greenhouse Diseases

There are various common diseases you may come across while tending to your garden. Some of the sources include infected plants from outside, carried in by insects or floating in the air. The following sections will outline some of these diseases in more detail.

Fungus

Wet conditions or overwatering can cause fungus

diseases like phytophthora, powdery mildew, root rot, and botrytis. You should monitor the moisture and humidity level in the greenhouse to avoid conditions that favor breeding of fungus.

Ensure there is proper drainage of containers and other potting media and do not leave plants soaked in water for a long time.

When fungi infect plants, the plants start to wilt and discolor. Sometimes, they may have fuzzy growth on their stem and leaves, which may later turn yellow in color. If the infections affect only the surface of the plant, you can apply neem oil and increase air circulation in the area. If the fungi affect the plant tissue, you should remove the plants from your garden and discard them far away. It is difficult to treat tissue-affected plants.

Bacterial Diseases

Some bacterial diseases that affect plants include Erwinia and bacterial blight. It is not easy to cure these diseases, and if they infect your plants, you will have to get them out of the garden and destroy them immediately.

The infected plants will have water-soaked spots while its tissue melts into a sticky mess. If you notice any of these signs, remove them right away.

Bacterial diseases can spread to other plants through dirty tools, potting medium, and containers. Proper sanitation and increased air circulation are important factors in preventing the spread of bacterial diseases.

Viruses

Viruses occur in various forms and sizes and are brought inside the greenhouse by insects (thrips and aphids), which are classified as plant-feeding insects. Plants infected by a virus have a yellow color or mosaic patterns on their leaves. If you notice any signs of a virus infection on your plants, you should take them out and destroy them immediately.

Always monitor your greenhouse for insects and treat your plants when they appear as soon as possible.

For any pest and disease control mechanisms to succeed, you must:

- Understand the various components of greenhouse diseases.

- Understand the different sources of the diseases you're facing; that is, are they caused by organisms or influenced by the conditions in the greenhouse?

GREENHOUSE

- Understand the different symptoms of all the pathogens. Know signs of root rot, symptoms of bacteria and virus affected plants and those of mildews, as knowing them will help you decide which pesticide or control mechanism to apply.

- Know the resistance mechanisms of the pests and fungi.

To control root rots in the greenhouse, you need to:

- Remove the infected crops.

- Sterilize the potting media.

- Wash your hands with soap to avoid spreading pathogens to other areas.

- Control the irrigation system to have a moderate soil moisture. The potting medium used should have adequate drainage to avoid waterlogged crops, and you should also make sure you are not overwatering the crops.

- Use the right fungicides to prevent seedling infections.

You would control powdery mildew pests by:

- Reducing the greenhouse's humidity.

GREENHOUSE

- Removing dead plant debris or material.

- Using fungicides to prevent the spread of infections.

If the irrigation water is the one causing pathogens, you should decontaminate the water through chemical treatment, filtration, or an irradiation method.

Chapter Summary

Controlling pests and insects affecting your crops in the greenhouse increases the productivity of the crops. Farmers use integrated pest management techniques to identify the types of pests affecting the farms and come up with the appropriate methods to control and prevent those pests.

You can solve most pathogen problems by maintaining good greenhouse hygiene, using disease-free plants, controlling the growing environment, and controlling entry to the greenhouse.

Other control methods you can implement include using biocontrol and chemical control and sanitizing the greenhouse environment. Successful control of pests and diseases requires you not only to discern the pest or disease affecting the plants, but also know the symptoms for each disease.

Diseases in the greenhouse are attributed to various sources of living organisms. Although there are other sources, these are the most common when figuring out the cause of pathogens and diseases in the greenhouse. Every greenhouse farmer should know the various sources and use that knowledge to come up with measures on how to prevent these pathogens.

In the next chapter, you will learn about various mistakes to avoid.

CHAPTER NINE

MISTAKES TO AVOID

The success of the farm produce is the dream of every farmer. However, there are many mistakes most beginners make when cultivating fruits and vegetables in their garden.

Learning about the mistakes that others made will help you not commit the same when you're in the initial stages of your gardening activities. Learning ahead contributes positively to the success of your farm and enables you to harvest healthier and tastier plants.

Site Selection

You cannot set a greenhouse in just any random place—you need to identify a good spot with a good drainage system. An area with a good slope is ideal for draining water in the greenhouse, and the greenhouse floor should be porous to allow water to drain properly. Floors made of gravel will do well in draining water.

A poor drainage system will result in waterlogged areas, which will be a breeding place for pests and other diseases that can affect your plants.

Setting Up the Greenhouse Away from Excess Shade

You must build your greenhouse in an area that receives less shade from tall trees and other buildings around. Excess shade will limit lighting, which is essential for plant growth in the greenhouse. Tree branches may also fall on the greenhouse and cause serious damage.

Plants also need protection from extreme heat during the summer months; therefore, installing a greenhouse that has shading material to shade the plants from the hot sun is a much better idea than placing a greenhouse otherwise.

Choosing the Right Plant to Grow in the Garden

You need to choose the right plant to grow in the greenhouse; for example, growing fruits together with vegetables may affect them. Fruit plants' height cause shade, which can affect the growth of other vegetables or crops grown in the same greenhouse. You must make sure you grow your fruits and other tall plant trees separately from other plants and vegetables.

Note that not all plants do well in a greenhouse, and some plants will need an open field to maximize their yield.

Humidity Inside the Greenhouse

High levels of humidity will encourage growth of mold spores and other diseases, which will affect your plants. You need to know the humidity needs of your plants and control the humidity level in the greenhouse to favor your plants' growth. Plants that need the same humidity levels should be growth on the same section.

Place Growing Bags and Pots in a Garden Stand

Putting growing bags, pots, and other basic greenhouse tools on the floor can encourage the growth of pests beneath the pots and growing bags. Garden stands allow you to arrange your pots on a double or triple step stand, thus creating more space in your greenhouse. Using stands can help you maintain good hygiene within the greenhouse.

You should always adhere to proper hygiene in the greenhouse to discourage weeds and pest infections from growing and becoming issues.

Excess Watering

Avoid overwatering plants in the greenhouse, as the humidity inside is controlled and there will be less water evaporation from the greenhouse soil. The excess water on the plants will encourage fungal infections and other diseases in the greenhouse.

Follow proper watering schedules and create a set watering schedule for yourself, in which you water at the same time every day.

Poor Pollination or No Pollinators Inside the Greenhouse

You have to plant floral plants near your greenhouse to attract pollinators to the surrounding area and eventually to your garden. Pollinators are attracted to the color yellow, so planting plants like marigold will attract them.

In some cases, there may be few to no insect pollinators in the greenhouse, thus affecting the pollination process. In this situation, hand pollination is essential for pollinating vegetable plants.

Failure to Expose the Garden Soil to Direct Sunlight

You need to expose the soil and the potting mixture to direct sunlight; otherwise, it will attract pests and maggots into the greenhouse. Exposing the soil inside to direct sunlight will kill most of these pests and fungal diseases. Don't make the mistake of leaving your soil out of the sun, especially if you are in an urban area. Make sure there is direct sunlight to kill the pests in the soil.

Pest Management

Most farmers don't pay close attention to their vegetables and plants and they fail to notice the slight changes in their plant until the pest has already damaged some plants and spread to other parts. Daily monitoring is essential to identify and pest infestation at its initial stages. This will make it easier to identify any infection and take appropriate measures before it spreads to other plants.

Crop Rotation

Another mistake many farmers make is planting the same crop in the same place for several seasons. Crop rotation is essential for success of any farm production.

GREENHOUSE

After harvesting a single crop, plant a different crop in that location, as this will help retain the soil's fertility and nutrients, resulting in healthy plants.

Heating

Don't buy the regular home heater for your greenhouse, as home heaters are not designed for moist environments. Buy rated heaters specifically designed for greenhouse and use them to regulate the winter temperatures. You should also use a rated power cord and an outdoor surge protector.

Fertilizers

Before applying any fertilizer to your plants, study the feeding patterns of the plants and its requirements. Each plant has different requirements beyond the general all-purpose fertilizer. Vegetables need fertilizer specifically formulated for use in the greenhouse. For example, tomatoes require a specific amount of fertilizer that is made for them, and how you would apply that fertilizer will depend on the instructions on the product label. Your studies will guide you in applying the right fertilizer and the right amount of fertilizer.

If you have several plants in your garden, group them based on their needs (water, shade, and fertilizer). You should also note down the feeding requirements of the plants and mark them. You may learn of some plants that require a lot of shade, but their fertilizer requirement is different from the others in the same group. Studying your plants' requirements early, even before the growing season, will result into a successful garden and healthy plants.

Determine the fertilizer pH level. Tomatoes grown in a container require a pH level that ranges from 5.6 to 5.8 for maximum yield. A high or low pH level will affect the nutrient value in the crops and will also limit the plants from achieving their maximum yield potential.

Rely on a Problem Resolution Center

If you face challenges in your garden, you should ask for help from a professional educator. Taking pictures of the infected crops will help in the documentation of the problem and makes it easy for the educator to give advice if they can't make it personally to your garden.

Commercial greenhouses require you to hire an agronomist to come and investigate your farm on a monthly basis. Always seek for help or assistance if you notice something with your plants.

Chapter Summary

GREENHOUSE

If you're growing your own fruits, vegetables, and herbs to share with your family, there is more to cultivating these crops in a greenhouse. Knowing all the greenhouse mistakes to avoid is a great way to begin you gardening journey.

Continuous learning and improvement of your gardening activities will result to gardening success and eventually a healthy harvest.

GREENHOUSE

FINAL WORDS

Greenhouse structures are essential to extend the growing period. Whether building a greenhouse to plant crops for personal use or commercial use, there are a lot of benefits you can get. Before building a greenhouse, there are various factors you have to consider like site planning and the types of plants to have in the greenhouse.

Depending on your location, you have to choose the right place to install the greenhouse. The site you select should have a good drainage system and be away from excess shade. After site planning, you need to choose the type of greenhouse to install. There are various designs with different styles and sizes, so choose a greenhouse type based on your plants' needs, budget, and the location. Set up a good layout for the greenhouse for how you want to arrange the sections.

Once you install your greenhouse, the next step is to add all the necessary equipment required for its operation. When dealing with different plants, you will notice each plant requires different climate conditions such as heating, temperature, and lighting. If you're planning to have all-year-round crops and extend the growing season, having an enclosed structure will be ideal. Greenhouses allow the farmer to control climatic conditions and humidity to make the environment suitable for cultivating vegetables, herbs, and fruits at any time.

To control climatic conditions in the structure, you need to invest in lighting system equipment, ventilation equipment, temperature control, and heating equipment. You also need to have the basic equipment for operating the greenhouse, which includes pots, containers, and trays for planting seeds. You need to place these pots on shelves or in the greenhouse benches to create more space for other plants.

Remember to water the pots and seedling trays well for the seeds to germinate. A good water management system is essential in your structure, and you can decide to use drip irrigation or an automatic watering system. Whichever system you choose, you have to ensure there is a good drainage system to avoid having a waterlogged condition. Poor drainage may harbor pests and diseases in the greenhouse, and to an extreme extent, result in rotting of the plant roots.

Once you have placed all the equipment, tools, and accessories, you can go ahead and start cultivating your plants. You need to get seed-starting mixture to plant the seeds. Avoid using the normal potting soil, which may be infested with pests and other pathogens. Soil preparation is essential when deciding on what plants to plant, and vegetables and fruits will do well in different types of soil; therefore, you need to determine which

GREENHOUSE

type of soil is suitable for planting each.

Soil preparation involves determining the type of soil and its consistency, how to improve the soil drainage, determining soil nutrients and pH level, balancing the pH level, and adding more nutrients to the soil through fertilization. Based on this information, you can figure out which soil is suitable for your plants. The water requirements for your vegetables or herbs depends on the type of soil in your garden. Water your plants with care and avoid overwatering or underwatering them.

Once the seeds germinate, you may decide to transplant the seedlings to a bigger container or put them to their final growing place. As the plants grow, you can add mulch to boost the plant nutrients and prevent weeds from growing. Monitor the plants growth on a daily basis to identify any change on the plant leaves. Watching the plants daily will in noting the plants' progress and identifying any pests or diseases that may infect the crops. The information you gather can help you know when to remove infected crops before they spread the disease.

Pollination is essential for the production of the plants. Most greenhouses lack pollinators, so hand pollination will be important for your plants to produce fruits. Alternatively, you can plant crops that attract bee pollinators around your greenhouse and open the windows to allow them to enter inside to pollinate your plants. Insect-pollinated plants produce more fruit compared to self-pollinated plants, and different vegetables, fruits, and herbs rely on different methods of pollination to produce fruits.

For all the plants to give you the maximum yield, you must have proper management of the greenhouse. Different plants do well in different seasons, so always know which type of vegetable of fruit you can grow in summer or during the busy spring season. Knowing when and what to plant during each season will play a huge part in your greenhouse's success. You also need to know how you can prepare your greenhouse for the winter season.

Proper maintenance of the greenhouse involves maintaining good greenhouse hygiene, weed control, and pest and disease management. You need to identify the various pests that can affect your greenhouse, their symptoms in the infected plants, and what causes them. It's only after determining the pest's sources and signs when you can come up with preventive and control procedures.

You should evaluate and document the control procedures you take for future decision-making. Regular monitoring of the crops, fertilization, and watering will result to healthy and productive plants.

You also need to remember the various mistakes others have made before you and that you may face while growing your plants. Learning ahead will enable you to avoid some of these mistakes, and continuous learning and improvement of your gardening activities will result to gardening success, and eventually, a healthy harvest.

www.ingramcontent.com/pod-product-compliance
Lightning Source LLC
Chambersburg PA
CBHW050311120526
44592CB00014B/1863